THE ESOTERIC PHILOSOPHY OF LOVE AND MARRIAGE

by

Dion Fortune

Albatross Publishers
Naples, Italy
2019

*Originally Published in London by
William Rider & Son, Limited 1924*

ISBN 978-1-946963-24-6

©2019 *Albatross Publishers*

Contents

THE ESOTERIC PHILOSOPHY

The Esoteric Philosophy of Love and Marriage

INTRODUCTION

THIS book upon the esoteric teaching concerning sex is addressed primarily to those who have no occult knowledge of the subject, but are seeking with open minds for information that may help them to solve the problems of life. To these it may be said, by way of explanation of the present treatise, that every race has a traditional secret wisdom which is never made public, but handed on by word of mouth and manuscript to those who are considered worthy to receive it. This tradition stretches back in an unbroken line to the remotest antiquity, the streams of different racial traditions converging as they approach their source.

The first section of the book is devoted to a brief outline of the esoteric doctrines in general, in order that the more detailed account of their teachings concerning sex may be comprehensible.

The reader is recommended to grasp the leading ideas here put forth, and then to try to express his own experiences and observations concerning life in the terminology herein employed and see how far they are thereby rendered illuminating. Let him

1

reflect that, if these ideas are true, certain results will ensue from contemporary occurrences. He should then watch for events in fulfilment of his anticipations or the reverse. In this way he will learn as much about the practical application of the esoteric teachings as is possible for one who is not an initiate of any of the fraternities that hold the secrets of occult science.

To those who already have a knowledge of esoteric matters some explanation is also needed, for the best-known books upon the subject have repeatedly stressed the danger of any form of sex-magic and pronounced it in all its forms to be uncompromisingly black and of the left-hand path. This, as anyone who has had practical experience of the matter cannot fail to be aware, is absolutely true concerning certain aspects and applications of this great force upon its passional side ; these aspects are touched upon in the latter part of the book in order that the unwary may be warned to avoid them.

The Western occultist, however, diverges from the Eastern tradition as popularly expounded in this country when he asserts that the sex-forces, in their higher aspects, are powerful regenerative agents ; these aspects are entirely divorced from physical function and are of the mind and spirit. Mme. Blavatsky, in that classic of occultism, *The Secret Doctrine*, refers to this in the following words, page 449 of Vol. III. :—

" For the production of alchemical results such as the Elixir of Life and the Philosopher's Stone, . . .

the *spiritual* help of the woman was needed by the male Alchemist. But woe to the Alchemist who should take this in the dead-letter sense of *physical* union. Such sacrilege would become Black Magic and be followed by certain failure. The true Alchemist of old took *Aged* women to help him, carefully avoiding the young ones ; and if any of them happened to be married they treated their wives for months both before and after their operations as sisters."

Though the doctrines of the Eastern and Western schools of esoteric science are practically identical, their methods in training initiates are fundamentally different, working, as they do, upon different Rays and under different Masters. No disparagement is contained in this statement; all Rays (in the occult sense of the term) proceed from the Divine Sun. The Eastern tradition has a magnificent literature and has grown and spread into a great tree, over-shadowing the life of the races that dwell under it, and honoured by all, even those who understand it least. The Western tradition has lost nearly all its ancient documents during centuries of per-secution, but it still holds the Keys of the Gate and can open it to those who seek.

The Eastern and Western schools differ greatly in their attitude towards those forces and facts of life which we sum up under the name of sex. To the Eastern, woman is an inferior, less highly developed in every way ; many Westerns regard her, on the contrary, as superior to man, the in-spirer, the guardian of the ideal. These different attitudes find their reflection in the esoteric methods of each tradition. The Eastern occultist seldom finds in purdah-dwelling women developments of intellect and spirit compatible with comradeship in his lofty and exacting work, and in such work, if sex cannot be used in its higher aspects, it must be eschewed altogether ; therefore the Eastern tradition makes no provision for the esoteric contribution of the female sex to race-life. In the Western tradition, on the other hand, woman plays an important part, just as she does in its social and political life.

Whatever conditions may prevail among races that segregate their women, no one can afford to ignore the sex-element in the higher life of the Anglo-Saxon races. Many Eastern initiators have failed in their dealings with Western pupils through inability to appreciate the great importance of this element in the latter's lives. There may be sincere and lofty purpose and true wisdom to impart, but there is not always an understanding of the Western constitution. When the higher centres are awakened, they are apt to function according to the type of activity which the Western Ray has built up in the Western vehicle, and confusion ensues if the Ray and the vehicle are not both understood.

Not a great deal of information can be given in a book of this nature, but enough, no doubt, to serve as clues to those who are experienced. The nervous strain so common among those who study occultism is largely due to the failure to secure a proper distribution of the life-forces among the vehicles.

CHAPTER I

THE MODERN CONDITIONS OF MARRIAGE

A STATISTICIAN affirmed some time ago that in England 25 per cent. of married couples were permanently separated; 50 per cent. lived together without love, and 25 per cent. were happy. Thus only one-quarter of the marriages taking place in England fulfil the purposes for which they are entered upon, and a person marrying has but one chance in four of happiness. No one who observes the home conditions among his friends and neighbours will regard these figures as unduly pessimistic. It may, indeed, be questioned if the amount of enduring love to be found in married life should be estimated as high as 25 per cent.

In the United States, the country of easy divorce, it was stated that the percentage of happy marriages is as high as 50 per cent. Therefore it appears that a condition of misery or boredom is not implicit in the married state, but is due mainly to the selection of unsuitable mates; two people who made each other miserable may yet succeed (instructed by experience) in mating happily with other companions if their unfortunate union can be dissolved.

There are several admirable books now available which explain the physiology of sex-life to the non-scientific reader, and these have been of great value in lessening the mass of human misery that arises from ignorance; but they do not solve the whole problem, they do not tell us why two well-informed, healthy, human beings may yet feel that they have failed to realise the higher aspects of love, and so missed the best that life has to give; nor why two people, each highly esteemed in the circle in which they move, may have a devastating effect on each other without a single unkind word or selfish action, so that companionship means misery.

The intuitions of all humanity declare that marriage can hold the greatest good in life, but it is very rare to see that intuition justified; yet, when this occurs, so great is the happiness achieved, and so uplifting an influence does it exert in its immediate environment, that all the married misery seems outweighed by the completeness of this one attainment.

What line shall we take, then, with regard to the institution of marriage in civilised society? Shall we imitate the Greeks, who required of their wives nothing but the bearing of heirs, while they sought the companions of their heart and mind among free, unmated women, whom we should regard as courtesans. Shall we weaken the marriage-bond by greatly facilitating divorce in conformity with the American practice? Or shall we continue with our present scheme of things, and stake all on a single irrevocable choice ?

Each of these plans has its disadvantages. By the Greek system women of the highest evolution seldom gave children to the race, for the women of promiscuous habits are usually sterile. Moreover, the mothers of the nation, prized only for fecundity, were given little culture of either character or intellect, and were, therefore, unfitted for the training of their children, being themselves untrained. It is generally agreed nowadays that the influences of early childhood are extremely important in character-building, and that ignorant and inexperienced women cannot transcend their own natures and give to their children what they do not themselves possess. It is said that the failure of the Turkish nation to evolve a high standard of national character among its ruling classes is due to the backwardness of its harem-dwelling mothers, whereas the peasantry, who cannot afford to seclude their women, are of a much better type of character.

The American method of easy divorce seems at first sight to solve the problem, but until it has been tested for a century nothing but a provisional opinion can be expressed. It should be remembered that the great majority of middle-class citizens of Anglo-Saxon blood do not avail themselves of it very freely, it is the wealthy and the negro who supply the highest percentage of divorces.

The consequence of easy divorce among the wealthy seems twofold; firstly, the character of those indulging in it seems to be undermined, and there is a tendency to shirk responsibilities and take nothing seriously ; the depths of life and love are not found in easily broken unions, and sensuality is fostered. Secondly, the children of divorced couples have no home-life of systematic training and discipline ; a step-parent, however conscientious, cannot replace one to whom the child is flesh of his flesh ; and all who have worked out the problem of bringing up an orphaned family know that nothing can replace the influence of a mother during childhood, or of a father during adolescence, and that the child deprived of either parent enters life under a heavy handicap. In estimating the best conditions of marriage we must not forget the rights of those for whose well-being marriage was primarily instituted —the children.

Finally, as to the modern English system, statistics condemn it—it is not working well. The Anglo-Saxon standard of marriage is the highest in the world, also the most difficult to achieve. What shall we do then ? Shall we lower our standards, or shall we try to discover the laws which govern married happiness, and so regulate its conditions ? The American branch of the race has followed the former course, but the older branch clings desparately to its ideals.

It is in the hope that knowledge may help to alleviate conditions before desperate misery gives rise to desperate remedies that the following pages are offered to the reader. They are based upon the teaching given in one of the Western esoteric schools.

The reader is asked to endure patiently, unprejudiced by his ignorance, the technicalities of a strange philosophy, and to accept whatever light it throws upon his own life-problems.

CHAPTER II

THE ORIGIN OF MATTER

ESOTERIC science premises the existence of the Great Unmanifest, which may be conceived as a sea of limitless but latent force which underlies all things and whence all things derive their substance and draw their life. This concept corresponds to the exoteric concept of God.

Secondly, it conceives the outpouring of this ocean in a directed but limited stream; this corresponds to the exoteric conception of energy.

Thirdly, it conceives this now manifested energy, by the intersection of its lines of force, forming whirlpools, which, by the opposition of forces, lead to stability; these whirlpools of locked-up forces, gyrating about their own centres instead of driving straight through space, are the units of stability which, in their varying combinations, form the different kinds of matter.

Esoteric science recognises more forms of matter than are known to physics and chemistry. It distinguishes, firstly, the original vortices of stability; secondly, their combinations into seven simple types of molecules; thirdly, it conceives combinations of these molecules into denser and more complex structures; and fourthly, the further combinations, of which these relatively complex structures form the units. In fine, it distinguishes the prime atom of manifestation arising from the Great Unmanifest and seven types of molecules, and these great divisions of matter, as known to esoteric science, are called the Seven Planes of Manifestation, of which the matter that composes our material world, and which alone is known to the exoteric scientist, forms the densest and most inert subdivision, and the latest to be formed in evolutionary time. Thus it will be seen that the esoteric scientist has for his studies a manifested universe seven times as great as that cognised by the exoteric scientist.

These seven planes, while all arising from the Unmanifest as First Cause, are conceived of as having immediate causal relations among themselves; thus the first plane to develop gives rise to the second and determines its manifestations, and the second to the third, and so on, down to the final plane of physical matter, which may be called the Plane of Effects, whereon the results of activities on the subtler planes may be observed and their consequences are finally reaped. It will thus be seen that the esoteric scientist acquainted with the laws of one of the higher planes could control conditions on all planes lying below it, being in his turn controlled by anyone who was master of a plane superior to his own. The final control is regarded as vested in the inherent nature of the Prime Manifestation.

It is the aim of that branch of esoteric science which is popularly called Magic, to obtain control of conditions upon one plane by acting upon the forces of the plane immediately above it, which acts as causal plane to the lower one. White Magic is distinguished as that exploitation of knowledge which aims at harmonising and uplifting existence along the lines of advancing evolution, and which, though it may concentrate its efforts upon a particular point, excludes from its benefits nothing which by its nature is capable of receiving them. Black Magic may be defined as that use of superior knowledge which endeavours to cause any section of existence to return to a phase of evolution below that to which it has attained, or which attempts to benefit any special section of manifestation at the expense of the rest.

CHAPTER III

THE ORIGIN OF MAN

ESOTERIC science, having conceived the first or Atomic Outpouring of force, of which the unit of manifestation is the primal vortex or so-called atom whose development forms the matter-substance of each plane of manifestation, next conceives a second or Monadic Outpouring, of which the unit of manifestation is the Monad, or spark of Divine consciousness, whose evolution leads to the development of the human soul and the heights of spiritual grandeur that lie beyond it. This Monad, or spark of spiritual consciousness, is conceived as forming about itself a body built out of the atoms of the plane below that upon which it comes into manifestation ; this body is formed upon the lines of force inherent in the spiritual Monad in the same way that the particles of a crystalline substance in solution build themselves up along the lines of force of the parent crystal ; for the ensouling life determines the configuration of the body.

Each plane is, comparatively speaking, a plane of free-flowing life-force as compared to the relative density of the plane below, out of which it builds a vehicle in which to confine its energies so that they may be directed to specific ends. The Monad, then, as an unconditioned life, builds itself a vehicle of the matter of the plane below that of its own substance ; this vehicle, however, though material when compared to the density of the plane of its ensouling life, is non-material when compared with the plane below it, and this newly-formed two-matter unit can build itself another and yet more conditioning body of manifestation on the next lower plane ; and so the building up of vehicles goes on, each giving a greater definiteness to the expression of the indwelling life, each laid down, metaphorically speaking, in concentric layers of accretion about the nucleus of the spiritual Monad until the final form is developed upon the material plane, the physical body as we know it.

A human being, therefore, is regarded by esoteric science as a sevenfold creature, not merely a duality of mind and body ; he is considered to have a vehicle built out of the matter of each plane of manifestation, subject to the laws and conditions of that plane, and capable of functioning thereon and nowhere else.   Each vehicle is built about and controlled by the vehicle of the plane above, and the core of all, the Monad, derives its substance from the Unmanifest as from an infinite reservoir of constant pressure.

CHAPTER IV

THE EVOLUTION OF MAN

WE have learned that the Monad builds up its bodies out of the matter developed upon each lower plane in the course of the first Outpouring : we have next to see how it learns to use those bodies. At the beginning of its evolution it grows by accretion, as the mineral kingdom does, adding body to body until the last plane is reached, and it has a sevenfold form ; thenceforward it adds no more bodies, but grows in complexity, body by body, beginning with the organisation of the last to be developed, the physical body ; the latter, therefore, is brought to perfection while the subtler vehicles are still undeveloped, mere potentialities.

The Monad, as we saw, is a spark of Divine consciousness sensitive to the conditions upon its plane of manifestation ; as soon as it gathers about itself a vehicle of matter of the plane below its own, it obscures its consciousness of its own plane, but extends its consciousness to its vehicle ; and so it proceeds down the planes till the physical body is developed. Therein the buried Monad has direct consciousness of one plane only ; dim at first in the primitive organisation of the earliest cycle of evolution, and growing in clearness as sense-organs were evolved, till we have the wonderful capacities of the human eye and ear.

Next we begin to see another and yet more wonderful sense developing, sporadically, but in a constantly increasing number of individuals. We find people who are aware of subtleties which escape the five physical senses ; they are sensitive to the emotional states of their fellows, they may even be able to read their thoughts. This means that evolution is bringing about the organisation of the next body to be developed, and that its sense-organs are beginning to cognise the conditions of the plane to which they correspond. In this way evolution will continue to bring body after body into function until all seven bodies are organised and correlated and the Monad has complete expression.

CHAPTER V

THE Planes of Manifestation are commonly designated numerically, but they are not numbered from
above downwards in the order in which they come
into manifestation and in which order they have,
for clearness sake, been presented to the reader, but
from below upwards in the order in which they
become perceptible to the esotericist who is developing clairvoyance; and this nomenclature, being
the one established by custom, will therefore be
employed, so that those already familiar with the
subject may not be confused.

THE SEVENTH PLANE, also known as the
UPPER SPIRITUAL, the PLANE OF PURE SPIRIT, or
the PLANE OF ABSTRACT SPIRIT, is the first phase of
manifestation; it draws its substance and energy
direct from the Great Unmanifest, which (using
the pictorial method, the only method by which
esoteric science can be taught) may be conceived
as lying immediately above the seventh plane
and as being a reservoir of infinite potential force
which, when it becomes actual, is referred to as
being upon the seventh plane of manifestation.

Upon this plane there is no differentiation whatever, and it is the plane upon which " All are One, and One is All." It has but two characteristics, the first is absolute harmony, and the second a tendency towards combination among its particles. Upon this plane, at the beginning of an evolution, issues into manifestation the Monadic Essence in which may be conceived as floating those innumerable nuclei of life, the monads, which eventually develop into individualised human lives.

THE SIXTH PLANE, LOWER SPIRITUAL OR PLANE OF CONCRETE SPIRIT. In the course of ages of cosmic time, evolution brings the organisation of the monadic essence to the phase of the sixth plane. Hereon it is found to diverge into seven different tendencies, seven currents of outflowing, which are called the Seven Rays and are designated by colour-names, and it is held that the monads which may be conceived of as floating in each of these streams of spiritual tendency will evolve to their ultimate perfection by means of a different type of activity. This partiality does not imply a one-sided development, but that, although all elements must be present, one will predominate and give the keynote. The prime characteristic of the sixth plane is Tendency.

THE FIFTH PLANE, THE UPPER MENTAL OR PLANE OF ABSTRACT MIND, sees the development of QUALITIES in the monadic essence, and its differentiation into TYPES. From this point onwards it would no longer be justifiable to speak of the Monadic

Essence, for upon this plane the life-nuclei come into function, and Life becomes lives.

THE FOURTH PLANE, The Lower Mental or Plane of Concrete Mind, is characterised by finiteness which, while it limits, gives a definiteness which is lacking upon the higher planes ; it is the plane of concrete thought and is characterised by memory.

THE THIRD PLANE or Upper Astral is the plane of the emotions, and is characterised by response to attraction, the desire for union.

THE SECOND PLANE, Lower Astral or Psychic Plane, is the plane of the instincts and passions, and is characterised by the desire to attract or possess.

THE FIRST OR PHYSICAL PLANE is the material world as known by human beings incarnate in bodies of flesh and blood.

CHAPTER VI

THE SEVENFOLD MAN

It is obvious from the foregoing remarks that man is composed of substances drawn from each of the seven planes of existence; by means of these elements in his nature he contacts these planes, and, if he were without an element proper to any particular plane, he could not perform the functions appertaining to that plane. Thus, if a man were lacking in substance derived from the third plane he would be devoid of tender affections, incapable equally of feeling them himself or understanding them in others.

Each of the substances proper to the seven planes is organised according to the laws of its own plane, and is referred to in esoteric literature as a " body "; but the expression " state of consciousness " conveys a more exact impression of the esoteric meaning of this term. Let the reader, in order to grasp the implications of this esoteric doctrine, conceive himself as having, in addition to his physical body, which is built of the matter of the first plane and responds to its conditions, an organised system of instincts and the passions to which they give rise.

Let him also conceive himself, by means of the sympathetic induction of passion in himself (a common phenomenon), as able to perceive the passions of others ; then let him call this aspect of his nature his psychic or passional body, and conceive of it as functioning upon the second or lower astral plane.

Let him then conceive of his emotional nature as similarly organised and related to its own plane of existence ; likewise his reasoning faculties and power of abstract thought ; finally, his spiritual nature and that ultimate spark of divine life which forms the nucleus about which his individualised existence is built up.

Thus it will be realised that man has, as it were, seven different aspects to his nature, and that each of these aspects is referred to as a body by esoteric science.

The monad, in the course of its evolution, is conceived of as gathering about itself the matter of each plane, but long ages of experience and development are required before the masses of matter concerned become organised into definite bodies capable of functioning both subjectively and objectively ; in other words, ages pass before the forming bodies are sufficiently evolved to carry on the functions of their respective states of existence, and to be aware of external conditions on their own planes of manifestation.

The physical body both functions and is aware of its environment by means of direct consciousness, but in the average man this is the only body that has as yet obtained its dual development; in him, however, the second, third, and very often, in civilised races, the fourth plane bodies are sufficiently developed to be capable of functioning subjectively; but it is not common to find a fifth plane body developed, carrying with it the power of abstract thought; and still rarer is it to find a true development of the spiritual nature, as distinguished from emotional ideals appertaining to the third plane, which are often mistaken for true spirituality.

In a more evolved type of man, however, we may get a development of one or more of the subtler bodies which enable them to perceive their environment, by means of direct consciousness, in contrast to subconscious impressions, as is the case in the unevolved man.   Thus, instead of merely being influenced subconsciously by the emotional states of his fellows, "without knowing what is the matter with him," as is usually the case, the evolved man is fully conscious of the feelings of his companions.   Evolution is steadily developing the subtler bodies, as is proved by the fact that what is called psychism is increasingly common in its minor manifestations.

It is a little-understood fact concerning man's nature that, although a synthesis of all the states of consciousness is the highest form of existence, it is possible, by concentrating upon any one state of consciousness, to limit attention to that state alone, and by this means to perceive, as a world of its own, that plane of manifestation to which it corresponds. When he does this, a man is said to be "functioning in his astral body upon the third plane," or in his concrete mind upon the fourth; and while he is so engaged, the physical form, owing to the detachment of consciousness from its nervous system, is found to be in a state of trance.

Those who have the necessary knowledge deliberately entrance themselves in order to obtain extension of consciousness upon planes which they are otherwise unable to contact in the stage of development to which they have attained; but it is little realised the extent to which this expansion of consciousness takes place involuntarily in sleep among persons who have evolved a little beyond the average. The true aim of evolution, however, is not to segregate consciousness, but to correlate it; and the trance-method of transcending physical consciousness is merely a temporary expedient.

CHAPTER VII

THE ESOTERIC CONCEPT OF LIFE AND DEATH

ESOTERIC science asserts the eternity of life. Its central concept is conveyed in the word REINCARNATION, which implies an enduring unit of existence ensouled in a succession of transient bodies. In order to render this concept clear it must be remarked that the INDIVIDUALITY and the PERSONALITY constitute two distinct aspects of man. The individuality is composed of the three highest bodies, the spark of pure spirit of the seventh plane, the concreted spiritual nature of the sixth plane, and the abstract mind of the fifth plane ; these, once they have been evolved, are conceived of as enduring for an evolution and then being absorbed back into the Infinite as organised centres of radiation. The four lower bodies—the concrete mentality, the emotional nature, the passional nature, and the physical body—are regarded as temporary accretions of the matter of their respective planes which the Individuality employs as a vehicle, and which, collectively, are said to compose the Personality.

The Personality is built up in order to enable the Individuality, which is formless, to acquire experience in the world of form, and it is discarded as it wears out and its usefulness diminishes, the experiences through which it passed being absorbed by the Individuality as food for its development. Thus it is the Individuality which undergoes evolution in the course of the ages, whereas the many Personalities related to it merely develop, function, age, and die; but as each Personality is built up by an Individuality which has progressed, it is of a more evolved type than its predecessor.

The Individuality, then, is said to be the Unit of Evolution, and the Personality the Unit of Incarnation.

From the doctrine of reincarnation arises the esoteric theory of Destiny. The term Destiny, it may be mentioned, is synonymous with the term Karma employed in the Eastern schools.

A man's Destiny is held to represent the sum-total of the causes he has set going in past lives, which determine the conditions of the present; but fresh causes are constantly being introduced by the modifying action of the will, therefore Fate is not the inevitability which exoteric thought conceives it to be, but is a conditioning rather than a determining influence. True, some causes set going in the past may be so strong that no effort of the will avails to stay their course, and they have to work themselves out till their force is spent; but by his will a man may determine the reaction he will make to them, whether he will be crushed or purified, exalted by opportunity well used, or degraded by its abuse.

Esoteric science teaches, therefore, that although a man has to work out his problems in the condition in which he finds himself in any given life and in the limited sense of this short section of time, he has not got free will, yet he can so determine the causes that shall go forward into his future that he can make of himself whatsoever he desires.

CHAPTER VIII

EVOLUTION AND INITIATION

IT will be seen that esoteric science conceives of man as evolving from the subhuman to the human and then on to the superhuman, to the states of consciousness of the psychic, the inspired, and the illuminated. The great tide of evolution will take even the most debased on to the heights of spirit in the course of time, but as great a length of time must elapse for the consummation of this process as has already served to bring man to his present state of development. There is, however, a method of quickening evolution which is known as INITIATION, where through the deliberate use of his reason and his will a man can do for himself rapidly what evolution is doing slowly for all existence.

It is held that life did not issue forth simultaneously from the Great Unmanifest, but rather in a stream or procession, so that, although all go by the same path, some are ahead of others, and therefore reach high states of development while their brethren are either awaiting manifestation or are at low degrees of evolution. These Elder Brethren, whether still in the flesh or advanced beyond the stage whereat a physical body is worn, may, if actuated by the same philanthropy which makes us care for the weak and ignorant upon the physical plane, instruct and help those who are worthy of, and capable of benefiting by, such assistance.

Many of such individuals have already been trained by the Elder Brethren, and these disciples form the vanguard of evolution. They, in their turn, instruct others who are their successors, so that evolution may be compared to a flight of wild duck in which the strongest take the tremendous air-pressure at the apex of the wedge and the weaker spread out behind.

If a man's moral, intellectual, and spiritual natures are well developed, or, to use the esoteric terminology, if his subtler bodies are becoming organised, then he may be chosen by the Elder Brethren for special training. Instruction will first be conveyed telepathically to his subconscious mind, and, when he has progressed sufficiently far in this way, he will be placed in contact with pupils of the Elder Brethren upon the physical plane, who will teach and train him consciously by the ordinary means of that plane—the spoken and written word. Then, when he has made further progress, the Elder and Younger Brethren together, by means of the process known as Initiation, correlate subconsciousness with consciousness.

The reader, at this point, may ask how this contact with the Masters can be made ? Little can be said upon this point, for it is a matter of inner experience. It suffices to say that the desire, if strong enough and maintained long enough, will pierce the veil and effect the contact desired. Thereafter the path opens up as the pupil advances.

CHAPTER IX

THE ESOTERIC CONCEPT OF SEX

To understand the esoteric philosopher's concept of sex we have to remember that the world as known to him is seven times as complex as that known to the exoteric philosopher, for to the former the physical world is but one of seven planes of manifestation; the physical phenomena known to us as sex form but one aspect of a force that functions upon all these seven planes.

Even exoteric science is beginning to recognise that sex has an emotional as well as a physical aspect. Esoteric science declares that it has mental and spiritual aspects in addition to those under which it is usually recognised; and that upon each plane it expresses itself differently, functioning according to the laws of that plane, for all the elements of sex found on the seven planes, blent in right proportions, are essential to the highest kind of sex-life. Moreover, it is on the subtler planes that the sex-forces originate and are controlled. It is only by understanding the manifestations of sex and the laws that govern them upon these planes that we can hope to control their action in ourselves and society.

The esotericist does not use the term " sex " as we do ; he speaks of " life-force," which he conceives to be an energy of an electro-hydraulic type, a radiating and magnetising vibratory activity, similar to electricity, to which it is very closely related, yet capable of compression and of exercising pressure after the type of water-power.

This force he conceives to radiate from the Great First Cause, and therefore to be divine in its nature, expressing itself through the vehicles which the monads have built upon the different planes, and therefore conditioned by the nature of the plane on which it works, and further limited by the type and imperfections of each individual vehicle ; so that, although the life-force may undergo many transmutations and even be put to uses far removed from its original impulse, it is nevertheless divine in origin and nature, to be revered as sacred, and to be held by the individual through whom it is functioning as a sacred trust which he has to administer under the direction of the Divine Life Itself, with the entire species of which he is a member as beneficiary.

This life-force maintains in existence all that is, and preserves living forms from the disintegrating forces that constantly seek to reduce all specialised substance to its common root ; this is the first function of the life-force—to maintain in manifestation that which has achieved a form, and to hold it at the level to which it has evolved.   When functioning thus it is known as Life the Preserver, and is conceived of as a unity.   It has a second task, however, in the creation of new forms, and for this it has to function in polarity as a duality with a positive and negative aspect, and it is to this phase of life-activity that the exoteric concept of sex is related.

For the maintenance of life a single force is sufficient, but for any form of creation two forces are necessary, one of which shall be actual and one inertly potential ; that is to say, the first force shall be a velocity and the second shall be a force locked up in form which shall be̅ set free by the stimulus of the velocity.

We have, then, in these two forces, one that is seeking to expend itself and so arrive at a state of equilibrium, and the other that is inert, potential, and awaiting a stimulus.   The latter or female-force may be compared to a charge of dynamite in whose particles chemical energy is stored up, latent ; and the former or male-force to the electric shock, or blow of a hammer, which releases that latent energy.

These two forces are spoken of by the esotericist as being positive and negative, male and female— the positive or male-force being the stimulator, and the negative or female force, by means of latent energy, performing the actual work of creation under the influence of the male or stimulator, and immediately becoming impotent when the impulse of his stimulation is withdrawn.   Wherever such action or reaction is at work the esotericist considers the relationship of sex is present, whether in the mineral kingdom or the world of mind.

CHAPTER X

THE ESOTERIC CONCEPT OF MALE AND FEMALE

IT was said by One who knew that in the Kingdom of Heaven there is neither marrying nor giving in marriage ; this is erroneously supposed to mean that the spiritual man is sexless. Esoteric science, however, conceives him not to be sexless, but on the contrary, bi-sexual, and therefore complete in himself. The individuality is two-sided, positive and negative, has a kinetic aspect and a static aspect, and is therefore male-female or female-male, according to the relation of " force " to " form " in its make-up. The personality, however, is one-sided, and therefore has a defined sex. The individuality may be thought of as a magnet, having a positive and a negative pole, one of which at a time is inserted in dense matter, and the nature of the pole inserted determines the sex of the body that is built up around it.

The individuality, whose life is an evolution, has both aspects to its nature ; but the personality, whose life is an incarnation, has but one aspect in function, the other being latent or undeveloped. This is well illustrated in the bee, wherein the

34

manner of feeding determines whether sex shall be
developed or not, and also in the human form
wherein the characteristic organs of the other sex
are always present in rudimentary form, and may
even, in certain types of abnormality, attain considerable development if not actual function.

While sex is strictly determined on the physical
plane by *structural form*, on the subtler planes it
depends upon *relative force*, which is constantly
varying, so that two people who are male and
female on the physical plane may be constantly
shifting their polarity in their relations on the inner
planes.   Thus, should they be dealing with a matter
in which the man is pre-eminent, he will lead and
she will follow, but should conditions change and
the pair be working in a sphere in which she is pre-
eminent, then the polarity will shift and the woman
will assume the mastery : witness the exceeding
meekness of a· man when a baby is thrust into his
arms.   The one who feels the deepest will be male
on the plane of the emotions, and the one who knows
the most will be male on the plane of the mind,
regardless of the body in which each happens to
be incarnated.   As, however, the male body is
better fitted for the expression of a positive type of
force, the man will generally be male on the subtler
planes as well as the denser ; but if there is any
considerable inequality of force, then the woman
may be relatively male to her mate upon the inner
planes.   It must never be forgotten that maleness
and femaleness are always relative upon the inner

planes, and as the physical vigour of the individuals of a pair shifts about, so will the relative
sexuality shift with it, and a man may be pure male
in his relations with one woman, and pure female, or
negative, in his relations with another. Form
determines the sex of the individual on the physical
plane, but *relative* force determines it on the inner
planes ; and this fact is the clue to much.

CHAPTER XI

THE INTERACTION BETWEEN POSITIVE AND NEGATIVE UPON THE NON-PHYSICAL PLANES

(a) *The Spiritual Planes*

" UPON the seventh plane All are One and One is
All." This is an oft-repeated axiom of esoteric
philosophy. Upon this plane exist entities of two
types : those that have as yet progressed but little
beyond their origin, and are upon the downward or
outgoing curve of evolution ; and those who, having
completed their evolution, have risen up to the level
of their source. This plane, we are told, is entirely
formless ; entities of the former type have not yet
achieved form; while those of the second, having
learnt all that form can teach them, have cast it
aside, together with its limitations, and attained to
perfect freedom within the limits of the universe to
which they belong.

All are one upon this plane, we are told ; the
relationship existing between each unit and the rest
of the plane far exceeds in intimacy and completeness the highest that is ever attained by earthly
lovers in their most ecstatic moments of union;

this state is the permanent, normal condition of
the seventh plane, which may well be called the
kingdom of heaven, for it is a state of perfect love
and perfect harmony. Human lovers fear that
they may lose each other in what they conceive to
be a vacant formless Nirvana ; on the contrary, the
perfection of union, which has hitherto only been
possible at rare moments between rare persons,
there becomes the normal state of the whole creation.

Upon the seventh plane, and upon the seventh
plane only, there is no differentiation into positive
and negative force. This plane has sometimes been
called the plane of pure pressure.

Upon the Sixth Plane occurs the first differentiation, or beginning of separateness. The universal
pressure of the seventh plane causes force to flow
forth in all directions, and the streams diverge as
they proceed. These streams are called, in esoteric
terminology, the Rays, and each ray is conceived
to be a special aspect of the Divine Nature. Each
monad, as it comes into being upon the sixth plane,
is found to have " issued into manifestation "
through one ray or another, and this primal environment determines the type of the monad for ever
after ; it will work with the forces of other rays,
but the colour-tone of its own ray will form the
keynote of its nature, and by the gate through which
it issued forth must it return when its cycle of
evolution is completed.

It is well known that for electricity to become
active it must flow in a circuit ; the man who is

completely insulated from all earth-contacts can touch a live wire with impunity, because he offers no channel for its force.   So it is with the life-force. It flows into each monad from the Divine source, and, having passed through that monad and ener-gised it, flows forth into circumambient space; then, having made a circuit which is only bounded by the limits of the manifested universe, and in the course of this circuit been reduced to its lowest form of manifestation, it is finally reabsorbed by the Divine as unorganised cosmic force.   If, however, it is desired to perform any work with this force, it must not be allowed to radiate into space and so become unavailable; it must be concentrated into a definite channel, and, by being limited and defined, be converted into pressure and thus made a source of energy.   This is achieved by causing it to flow and return in the channel of individualised form.   In the path of outgoing it makes its own channel through each and all of the individualised monads then in existence, but a path of return for it has to be made if its wasteful diffusion is to be prevented.   The knowledge of the methods of making this path of returning is one of the secrets of practical occultism.

The methods of achieving this flow and return are, in principle, the same upon all the planes, but the exact device employed differs according to the matter in which it is being carried out.   In essence it is this : a monad of a type inclined to press forward into manifestation or individualisation cooperates with a monad of a type inclined to press forward towards union with the Divine, towards a universalisation. If these two can meet together and form a continuity of substance, the life-force that is flowing out from the Divine through the positive or male individual, instead of radiating into free space after its work in the machine of his organism has been accomplished, will flow back to the Divine through the negative or female individual. At the point of junction between the two units the force can be tapped and rendered available for creation in the matter of the plane upon which the union is being effected. This is the essence of the esoteric teaching concerning the sex-function.

This device of cosmic sex, or polarity, if that word be preferred owing to the associations of the other, is resorted to upon the sixth plane : firstly, in order to induce a strong flow of force from the seventh into a sixth plane form ; and secondly, in order to maintain this force upon a high level and avoid the degradation and diffusion it would undergo if allowed to follow its normal course, run down the planes, and diffuse into cosmic space before returning to the Divine. An example will assist to make this clear. Let us take the case of a man of lofty spiritual character who feels himself called to a spiritual mission of regeneration to mankind. In the parlance of esoteric science it would be said that such a man, in order to be a channel for lofty spiritual forces, must have his sixth plane body highly developed, because he is working with the forces of that plane and they can only achieve adequate expression through a highly organised vehicle. If that man is content to remain a solitary devotee he may raise his own life to a very high degree of evolution by communing with the Divine Life, but he will make no mark on his race and age ; the outside world will be uninfluenced by him. Should he, however, choose to perform work in the outside world, to influence the spiritual life of his fellows, it will be observed that he immediately gathers about himself a little group of disciples who stand in a different relation to him than do the rank and file of his followers. To his followers he gives, and neither asks nor receives any return ; but on his disciples he depends in some peculiar and intimate way but little understood by the outside world. Though they are of lesser spiritual stature than himself, he yet leans upon them and is deeply affected by any defection on their part.

These disciples may be male or female, it matters not : all that is required of them is that they should be in intimate sympathetic union with their master, and of a degree of spiritual development approximating to his own, and then it will be seen that the little group functions as a unit at the core of the spiritual movement. Furthermore, should missionaries be sent out to spread the Master's teaching, it will be observed that they are sent in pairs in order that they may assist each other.

Now, in this interaction between a strong positive

nature, which acts as channel for a powerful spiritualising force and less vigorous, relatively negative natures which receive this force, the esoteric scientist would see the divine life-force functioning in polarity.

A curious confirmation of this statement will be seen in a phenomenon which not infrequently occurs in connection with the invocation of spiritual forces. Many a religious teacher founders upon the rock of sensuality, and those who succeed in steering the bark of life safely through the narrow strait of righteousness have left record in their autobiographies of terrible struggles before the victory was won. They were " tempted of the devil " to an extent which is spared the ordinary mortal; their sensual nature, to judge from the visions and thoughts that they record as assailing them, must have been as strong as their spiritual nature, and it was only by an extreme asceticism that it was kept under control. Hence mortification of the flesh, and the avoidance of all possible stimulation of fleshly desires, is a *sine qua non* of the higher forms of religious devotion.

Some psychologists see in this well-known phenomenon another proof that sex is at the root of all things, and regard the religious feelings as sublimations of the sexual ones, thinking that they have disposed once and for all of the spiritual life by proving its connection with the sexual life. The esotericist, however, views this phenomenon from a different standpoint. He believes both sets of activities to be the manifestation of one and the same force, a pure divine force of the utmost sacredness, and that the form which this force takes is determined by the machine through which it functions, so that, should this force be run through the vehicle of the sixth plane body, it will manifest itself as spiritual fervour and dynamic power, and will act upon the spiritual natures of those with whom it comes in contact; whereas, should it be run through the mental body, it will be creative intellect; and if through the physical body, sex-force in the ordinary sense of the term. Yet he holds that, wherever it runs, it is one and the same force, and that its final manifestation in procreation does not in any way degrade it, but that a force primarily spiritual being employed in procreation makes procreation itself a divine and sacred act.

Popular thought, however, and especially theological thought, frightened by the well-known phenomenon of the sensuality of the mystic, does not regard the life-force when manifested upon the physical plane as in any way a sacred thing, but rather as a manifestation of the lower side of our nature at war against our spiritual self; but there are some confessors, wise in human nature, who are shrewd enough to see it as different aspects of one and the same thing. When sensuality brings a religious teacher into disrepute it is usually considered that that man's life, as a spiritual force, is necessarily over; and this may, indeed, be the case, for should the great forces he was handling have so

slipped from his control as to come down to the
physical level, he will find it very hard, after such a
cloud-burst, to gather them back again into their
appointed channel ; his embankments may have been
swept away, and he may never again be capable of
the concentration of energy whereby work is effected.
But all the same it was a spiritual force that broke
bounds, and not a force of the underworld. The
tremendous cosmic energy which that man had
caused to flow through the channel of his individualised self proved of greater voltage, metaphorically speaking, than he could carry, and so his
spiritual nature fused under the strain and " short-
circuited." The current was literally earthed.
Instead of the strongly organised spiritual nature
keeping the current within its appointed channel
and handing it on to the spiritual side of others, so
that it should flow back to its divine source without
once leaving the sixth plane, the pressure upon that
man's spiritual body was so great that the force got
out of hand and followed the line of least resistance,
the line of the natural evolutionary flow, from the
seventh plane down to the first, and then back
again *via* the earth-soul ; and he was as little
culpable as is the man whose mill-dam gives way
and swamps a village. True, he ought to have
known that the head of water was too great for the
strength of his embankments, but he is not the
deliberate murderer of that village.

This is a phenomenon well known to the esoteric
scientist, the bursting of a spiritual mill-dam under

pressures too high for the organism to withstand, and the degradation of divine forces to the lowest planes of existence. What, it may be asked, is the remedy for this ? Firstly, prevention is better than cure, and all subtle forces should be carefully regulated to the moral stamina of the person employing them ; secondly, solitary work should be avoided so that other eyes may be able to see the first crack in the mill-dam, a thing of which the owner thereof would be the last one to become aware. Then, should such a warning of collapse appear, the menaced individual should stop all inner activities and turn out on to the material plane in vigorous bodily exercise, or even mortification of the good old-fashioned type. Above all, he should refrain from invoking any more spiritual power till the channels for its passage have been repaired. For the mystic to invite further ecstasies under such conditions is to induce either an outbreak of sensuality or an outbreak of hysteria, and the intuitions of many spiritual souls were sound when they felt that under such circumstances they were unworthy to approach their God, but must work humbly in the fields, or tending the poor, till they had rendered themselves worthy recipients of His favours and He deigned to approach them again. Such spiritual humility would save many a would-be saint from shame. When the life-forces are upon the lower planes we open up the higher planes at our peril.

(b) *The Mental Planes*

The action of polarity can be clearly traced in the two aspects of mind functioning as abstract and concrete thought. Upon the fifth plane, or plane of abstract thought, the great rays that represent the activities of the sixth plane are further elaborated into qualities and abstract principles. Being entirely abstract, this plane can only be conceived of with the help of similes, and its nature can be no more than indicated in a book of the present type. A practical illustration may assist, however, in showing the nature of the activities of this plane.

There are two types of logical thought. In the first or deductive type, from a general principle, particular instances of its operation are inferred; and in the second or inductive type of reasoning, a general law is inferred from particular instances. While everybody makes use of both these methods in mental work, it will be found that one or other type predominates in the logical thought of each individual sufficiently evolved to make use of this plane of mentation. The great bulk of humanity, as can be readily observed, have not reached this state of evolution, but proceed by the rule-of-thumb method, depending upon memory for guidance, and unable to draw more than the most obvious conclusions from experience.

Individuals upon the upper mental plane may therefore be divided into two types, those who are in possession of the great abstract principles of this plane and are aiming at their application to denser forms of existence, and, conscious of their source in the Divine, are anxious to pass on down the stages of evolution bearing the divine light with them ; and the other type, which, conscious of its goal in the Divine, is ever anxious to synthesise all experience into spiritual types. The one is a diffuser, the other a unifier ; the one functions with a male action, the other with a female action.

What will be the expression of these two types in actual life ? The one will be a philosopher, enunciating general principles, and from them inferring their consequences ; and the other will be a scientist, collecting masses of data and deducing general laws from his observations. Of course, in actual practice, each thinker should employ both methods. Were he merely a collector of facts, though such exist, or were he merely an enunciator of unverified principles, and such exist also (though modern education tends to stamp them out), he would achieve little eminence in the world of thought ; our greatest contributions to human knowledge have been made by the philosophic scientist or the scientific philosopher.

In general practice, however, one type of mind collects the data and another type philosophises upon that data, and only in the most eminent do the two activities work together. In this co-operation the esoteric philosopher sees the activity of the two types of polarity, the male induction and the female deduction, and would declare that these two methods of activity are as necessary for creation upon the plane of abstract thought as upon the plane of dense matter, the one without the other being sterile, whereas the two functioning together bear the fruit of new knowledge.

Upon the fourth plane, the plane of concrete mind, the principle of polarity again applies. How weary and difficult is intellectual work performed in solitude without appreciation or sympathy, but mind responds to mind with renewed stimulation and activity when there is a mutual fund of knowledge. All brain-workers know well the sudden bound forward of inspired effort after a conversation, a correspondence, or even the reading of a book upon the subject in which they are interested. The stimulative reaction of one upon another can be very clearly seen upon this plane, and whether they understand its implications or not, brain-workers know it well by experience and make great use of it, as can be observed in the records of their lives. The esotericist likewise knows this principle and avails himself of it ; indeed, for certain types of work he has to wait for his counterpart, and cannot proceed alone.

(c) *The Astral Planes*

The planes of the emotions and passions are known to esoteric science as the upper and lower astral respectively, and here we can trace the beginnings of sex as it is ordinarily understood.

Upon the third plane or upper astral, the plane of the tender affections, we see the emotional side of the nature desiring an object for the expression of its feelings or the fulfilling of its needs, and these two aspects of feeling the esotericist would regard as emotion in polarity. Upon the third plane there is still no fixity of sex; the mode of functioning determines whether the force in question is positive or negative, of a male or a female type. That which has a need of emotional expression is regarded as male, and that which has a need of emotional satisfaction is regarded as female. These modes of functioning, however, can occur in rapid sequence, or even simultaneously in respect of different aspects of the nature, and the polarity is therefore constantly fluctuating. This fluctuation of polarity upon the upper astral is a very important factor in the practical application of these principles to human affairs.

Upon the lower astral or plane of the instincts, polarity tends to become more stable, because this plane is very closely linked to the physical, and its conditions are influenced by the physiological phases of the body; but strange as it may appear at first sight, the sex of the second plane body is the opposite of that of the physical body. It is not difficult, however, to give the reader evidence of the truth of this statement. It is well known that a woman's love is steady, enduring, but of less intensity than a man's, whereas he reacts violently to a stimulus, and reverts to a passive condition when the stimulus is withdrawn; in this the esotericist would see the steady flow of force through the positive male

4

vehicle of the woman, and the sudden explosion of latent energy in the female desire-vehicle of a man under the stimulus of a kinetic force.

Upon this plane certain kinds of magic are worked in which sex-force is made use of. Hence one danger of ignorant trafficking in unknown quantities and the need of great self-control on the part of those who embark upon such occult studies. Anyone who is acquainted with those circles in which the study of practical occultism is cultivated knows that there is constant trouble in this respect unless a high moral standard is maintained.

CHAPTER XII

POLARITY UPON THE PHYSICAL PLANE

WE are equipped with physical bodies in which the configuration of the generative organs determines the part we shall play in the polarity of life ; we are born male or female and have to abide by the decision of our conception, the phenomena of the hermaphrodite and homosexual being regarded as pathological by the esoteric as well as the exoteric scientist.

The control of sexual activity upon the physical plane is determined by the chemistry of the endocrine organs, the ductless glands that pour into the blood secretions known as hormones, which, circulating in the blood-stream, stimulate the secretory organs to activity. Thus the sex-pressure rises and falls in an individual according to the chemical composition of his blood which is constantly fluctuating within certain limits. Charts have been worked out to prove this ; the monthly cycle of a woman's sex-life has been shown to coincide with the percentage of lime-salts in her blood, and in the male also there is a rhythmic rise and fall of desire which, however, has been less studied than the more marked periodicity of the female.

It has been declared by certain popular writers that in this discovery we have the clue to the whole of life, emotional, intellectual, and spiritual. It has even been stated that a man is simply the synthesis of his endocrines, and that every spiritual impulse, every emotional ideal, can be expressed in terms of lime-salts. One point, however, is ignored by these philosophers of the physiological, and that is the profound influence on the endocrine organs of emotional states. One school of physiology declares that the adrenal glands situated over the kidneys are the controllers of the sex-functions; another school calls the adrenals the organs of combat, as it is their secretion which tenses all the tissues to readiness for violent exertion and causes the blood to clot freely if wounds should be inflicted, and it is known that these organs are stimulated to activity when their owner feels the *emotion* of anger or fear. It will thus be seen that exoteric science is proving experimentally what esoteric science has long taught—that the functioning of the physical organism is controlled from the plane of the instincts and passions. Although the chemistry of the endocrines controls the functioning of the physical tissues, the endocrines are themselves controlled by the emotions.

There is no need, in a book of this nature, to go into the well-known details of sexual physiology; enough has merely been said to indicate the point where exoteric meets esoteric science, that point being the endocrine system.

CHAPTER XIII

POLARITY WITHIN THE ORGANISM

IN the foregoing chapters the facts of polarity between units of opposite types functioning upon the different planes has been briefly explained; there is, however, a secondary type of polarity known to esoteric science that occurs within the individual itself. The several bodies or principles of man are relatively positive and negative in their relations to each other, the more subtle being positive in its relation to the more dense. Thus, the psychic body, the body of instincts and passions, is positive towards the negative physical body, stimulates it to activity and determines its conditions, subject, of course, to the laws of physics and chemistry that control the material plane.

Each body in the series, then, is controlled by the one above it, and has to await the stimulus of this subtler body before it can function; likewise, it acts as controller to, and stimulator of, the body below it in the line of manifestation. It is therefore male in relation to its denser vehicle and female in relation to the subtler matter that ensouls itself.

The seventh plane monad or spark of spiritual

life is the prime determinant of the whole septenary ; it gives life and individualisation, without which there would be no unit at all. The sixth plane ray conditions determine type ; and the fifth plane abstract qualities, in combination with the ray-type, determine the individualised nature of fundamental traits.

From the fourth plane downwards the personality is built up by means of experience, for it is upon the fourth plane of the concrete mind that memory begins. The individuality of the three upper planes, however, entirely determines the original direction of the path pursued in evolution ; whatever modifications may occur as the result of circumstances, the individual will always tend to revert to its original line of advance as soon as opposition is removed.

The memories collected in the concrete mind naturally determine the emotional reactions an individual makes to his environment upon the third plane, and his feelings will equally determine the goals of his instinctive activities upon the second plane, making him seek that which is pleasant and avoid that which is unpleasant.

The first plane, as we have already seen, is regulated by the emotions playing upon the endocrines and the impulses given to the nervous system.

We may then say, to sum up, that each body is *governed* by the laws of its own plane, and that its functionings are *regulated* by the body of the plane immediately above its own. Thus, the physical body being controlled by the psychic body, we should seek to influence that body if the control of the physical machinery should go amiss. This we do from the third plane, which is the plane of picture-consciousness, by causing it to dwell upon images of health and perfect functioning; these pictures, if they arise with sufficient clearness and persistency in the picture-consciousness of the third plane, will pull the second plane body into line, and cause it to send corresponding impulses to the dense vehicle, which, as soon as the poisonous chemical combinations arising from faulty functioning can be expelled from the system, and provided no organic change has taken place, will then revert to conditions of health.

This remedial process has been popularised by the system known as auto-suggestion, and a more elaborate and far-reaching application of it has been made by Christian Science, wherein the fifth plane aspect of the mind is induced to dwell upon abstract principles of harmony, and control assumed from that plane. When true spiritual healing occurs, as contrasted with so-called spiritual healing arising from the auto-suggestion of religious faith, it takes place from the seventh plane itself, the monad assuming control of all bodies below it and determining their conditions, an exceedingly rare occurrence.

In the ordinary course of nature the mutual control of the series of vehicles goes steadily on, but the man who wishes to raise the forces of any

particular body to a high potentiality can deliberately avail himself of it.   Supposing the man we are
considering is a creative artist, he can raise the
potentiality of his astral body (for it is upon the
third plane that the imaginative arts are carried
on) by bringing to bear upon it his intellect in
addition to his imagination.   He will find that
the application of the concrete mind to the
problem of a half-visualised work will cause his
emotion to concrete itself into an artistic form, a
concretion that would not have taken place had
nothing beyond the emotional forces of the third
plane fired him.

Equally, upon the fourth, or plane of concrete
thought, he must bring into function his power of
abstract mentation if he is to see the implication of
the facts he is considering.   Abstract thought must
derive its stimulus from spirit itself.

This action and reaction between two of a man's
vehicles which is necessary for creative work, for
that externalising of the force within an individual
by providing for it a vehicle in the matter of one or
other of the planes, whether the vehicle be in the
form of the written word upon the mental plane,
or of sound or colour upon the astral, would be
regarded by the esoteric scientist as an example of
the everlasting principle of polarity underlying all
creative functioning.

A reverse flow of the current, however, is sometimes achieved; a man may seek to stimulate a
particular vehicle by means of the one below

instead of the one above ; thus, he may cause his concrete mind to throw his abstract mind into a state of activity. In this case we get the man who uses abstract principles in the service of particular instances, who demands that the laws of the universe shall fall in with his standards of right and wrong, who reads his own interpretations into the utterances of minds greater than his own and then presents them as justifications of his views. He is one-sided, bigoted, unamenable to argument, and unable to see any other side of the case than that which he has predetermined ; thus the nature of the lower plane limits the inspiration available through contact with the higher.

Equally, the man whose emotions prompt him to intellectual work is inclined to seek to prove a case rather than to discover the truth, and where the emotions are controlled by the appetites rather than the reason we have the unstable, inconstant, violent individual, " all things by turns, and nothing long," the sentimentalist, lacking the driving force and intelligence necessary to give effect to his dreams.

When the instincts are controlled by the physical sensations rather than the tender affections which should humanise them into love, we have the sensualist, cruel or voluptuous as his passions fluctuate with his endocrines.

Alcohol is one of the most potent factors in reversing the polarity of the bodies. Absorbed by the physical body, it speeds up the vital processes till the dense vehicle is more actively energised than the subtle bodies, and therefore becomes positive in its relations to them, and capable of giving the stimulus that sets them creating. When, however, the urge of the alcohol slackens, there is a period of " slack water " as the flow of the vital current comes to a stop before it can reverse its motion and resume its natural course. This constitutes one aspect of the reaction well known to follow upon the use of alcohol.

CHAPTER XIV

POLARITY WITHIN A GROUP

MODERN science is beginning to realise that the psychology of a crowd does not merely consist of the sum-total of the natures of the people forming it ; esoteric science has long known this truth, and made great use of it in its work ; ritual draws a large measure of its power from the fact that it focusses a group and draws upon the powers of the group-mind.

The theory of the group-mind, though well known to occultists, is but little familiar even to psychologists who have not studied this line of thought, therefore a brief outline must be given in order to render plain its special application to the subject of this book.

(Let me say, however, for those who are familiar already with the esoteric concepts in their exoteric form, that a group-mind is not the same thing as a group-soul.)

A certain portion of the subconscious mind is not walled up within the personality. When a number of people have their attention focussed upon the same object and feel towards this object the same emotion, as when a congregation's attention is concentrated upon a preacher with either love and admiration or resentment and hate, the free-floating portions of its subconsciousness tend to flow together and amalgamate in a single cloud which overshadows the whole group (it must be clearly understood that metaphorical language is employed). The composite mind thus formed will contain only those ideas and feelings which are directed towards the common object of attention ; these ideas will diffuse themselves throughout its substance and so find their way into the subconscious minds of all the people composing the group, and thence will influence their conscious minds. Hence the importance of a careful selection of membership in any closely organised group, for a single dominant personality can tinge the whole.

When a group-mind has become well established it has a distinct personality of its own. It is a separate entity, drawing its life from the group that brought it into being ; it can be altered by any alteration in the spirit of the group, but it can only be destroyed by dispersing the group, so that, should an undesirable tone make itself felt in an association of persons, the only remedy is to disband, and after an interval start afresh.

This group-mind, as soon as it is sufficiently developed, affiliates itself to those natural forces to which it is most nearly akin. For instance, a philanthropic group-mind will draw upon the spiritual forces of the faith that inspires it, and a patriotic one upon the group-soul of the race. Therefore, although individuals will find that their energies are drawn upon when they are engaged in building up a group-mind, they will find that when once it is built, it becomes a source of energy for them to draw upon in their turn.

A concrete example will serve to make this somewhat difficult and unfamiliar concept clear. Let us imagine a man with a spiritual message to deliver. By great effort he succeeds in gathering around himself a little band of believers. As soon as he has accomplished this he finds that his work has become much easier, he preaches with much greater force and influence, and less effort ; his inspiration becomes stronger and less spasmodic. Disharmony or indifference among his group will affect him very closely. Any minister of religion will confirm this from his experience of the dead-weight of an inert congregation and the inspiration of an enthusiastic one. Those most prominent in the work of the Church will be very definitely aware of the backing and momentum of the group-mind established by a common interest and enthusiasm ; it acts as a psychic flywheel to carry them over the dead-centre of personal shortcomings. To these people the group-soul acts as a male force, stimulating them in their creative activities and protecting them from external influences and antagonism.

In the case of the rank and file, however, the position is reversed, the group-soul draws upon them ; but by drawing their life-forces from them

it sets up a spiritual suction, as it were, and fresh
life-forces enter them from the universal life. One
of the principal causes of trouble in unmated
women is the stagnation and staleness of their unused life-forces ; the group-mind, by calling upon
these, prevents this stagnation and puts them in
circuit. It will invariably be observed that a religious or philanthropic movement draws a very
large portion of its power from the unmated women
who flock about it, because it supplies them with
an outlet for their energies. These women pour
into the group-mind those energies which would
have been spent in love and care for husband and
children had they been mated.

Thus the work of civilisation gets done, the group-
soul of the race absorbing the energies of a large
number of women into itself. It may be observed
that the tendency of all highly evolved civilisations
is to produce a superfluity of women, more than
can be absorbed in the task of reproduction ; these
women are produced of deliberate purpose, because
they are wanted for the group-work by means of
which the higher phases of evolution are brought
into manifestation.

By knowledge of this fact, and deliberate use of
its possibilities, the unmated woman can find her
place in the world, feel her idle energies being drawn
upon, and herself caught into the great stream of
psychic race-life, which is such a potent source of
inspiration and satisfaction to those who are taking
part in its flow.

A group-mind, then, has two aspects; it is a reservoir of force upon which the leaders of the group draw for their creative work, and it is an outlet for the unused and wasted energies of its rank and file. A knowledge of this fact offers a valuable contribution to the solution of the problem of our superfluous womanhood.

CHAPTER XV

THE IDEAL MARRIAGE

SELDOM is the ideal marriage seen, and yet each human being who enters upon that state does so in the hope that it will yield him the highest earthly happiness. Intuitively he knows that only in union with another being of an opposite polarity to himself can the full possibilities of human evolution be realised, and in the hope of attaining the highest evolution of which he is capable, he embarks upon a life of interaction with one of the opposite sex ; he stakes all upon a single venture, and seldom obtains thereby his soul's desire. Many marriages rest upon no other basis than mutual toleration ; many couples are only held together by the pressure of public opinion ; some are bound to each other by no higher bond than mutual convenience ; and yet each of them was led into the married state by the sense of a need which only union with another could fulfil.

This, then, is at the base of desire for union—a need, whether for the expression of an overflowing pressure of life or the reception of a force lacking to the nature—and only that union fulfils its purpose in which these needs are met, in which each of the pair finds in the other a demand for that which he craves to give, and a fulfilment of his own desires ; there has to be an interchange which takes from each his painful superfluity and uses it to supply the other with that which he lacks.

If this consummation upon all points be not achieved, then the craving for union will continue as an unsatisfied and tormenting hunger, or will turn elsewhere for its satisfaction, involving misery and social disorder. The alienation may be partial or total ; the individual as a whole may withdraw from his or her mate and seek another in an un-legalised union with all its dire consequences, or he may turn away with but a part of his nature, seeking intellectual companionship and emotional sympathy alone, and refraining from that act of physical union which popular thought alone recognises as a sexual act. It would, however, be rash to say that a man is any less male in his relations with a woman because he represses his desires towards her and contents himself with intellectual companionship alone. Jesus says that whosoever looketh upon a woman to lust after her hath already committed adultery with her in his heart ; and those who have insight into human nature know that they have more cause to be jealous of the loyalty of the mind than of the body ; a wife has little cause for pride in a tribute of the physical instincts which could be paid to any comely female of the species, if the deep yearning of the higher man in the

5

being she has married turns elsewhere. It is the woman who is the object of an illicit love who truly holds the man rather than she who shares his name and bed.

Our laws and theology, however, with a short-sighted policy, reckon of nothing but physical fidelity and ignore the lust of the eye, thereby building for us whited sepulchres full of all un-cleanness.

The laws of mating, as understood by esoteric philosophy, embrace much more than mere physical union, recognising, as they do, the seven bodies of man and sex, or polarity, upon each of the seven planes according to their several conditions. Eso-teric philosophy teaches, therefore, that unless a man mate each of his bodies which has arrived at a functionable state, his union will be incomplete, and he will still be in a state of sex-hunger, seeking his mate.

All men, however, are not equally evolved ; in the average man at the present day only the first three bodies are capable of mating—the physical vehicle, the body of the instincts, and the body of the emotions ; that is to say, he is capable of physical congress, of instinctive desire, and of tender affec-tion for his mate, but has little conception of in-tellectual companionship. A more evolved man, however, will have this latter ideal if his mental body be in function, and will seek for his wife one with like interests to his own ; a more primitive type, on the other hand, will demand of his mate nothing but a gratification of his senses, and will be quite indifferent to her when his passions are satiated.

Thus it will be seen that if a man who has three bodies in function and is capable of the tender affections marries a woman who has but two in function and has no concept of married life beyond passion and physical gratification, disaster will occur ; or should he, having four bodies in function, marry a woman who can only love and is not capable of being a companion to him, sorrow will also occur. The woman will derive from her husband all that she requires, for she is functioning up to her full three-plane capacity, but he will have an un-mated mental body which will assuredly seek a mate, and possibly find it in an intellectual woman capable of functioning upon the fourth plane, and then will be seen one of those platonic friendships of which everyone is instinctively suspicious, but which no one can convict of any offence against the laws of morality.

It will be found that no matter how loyal a man may be in will and action towards his wife, a union upon the higher plane will tend to divert the flow of the life-current so that it short-circuits across the fourth plane. Instead of passing down the vehicles of that man, till by means of the generative organs it be returned to the Divine through the completion of the circuit in the act of physical union with his wife, it will flow to his intellectual companion in the form of intellectual force. His feelings towards his wife will become as empty as the bed of a stream below the closed sluice-gates that have turned the water into another course.

It will remain to be seen whether the morality of the platonic friends can avail to keep the current in its appointed channel, or whether they will be shaken out of their platonism under the pressure of the life of the universe seeking expression. If their morality give way the life-forces will break bounds, and, following the line of their natural flow, run down the emotional and passional vehicles till they reach the physical. Then, and not till then, will what is legally known as misconduct at last be committed.

Let us now consider the case of a highly evolved man who is preparing to mate, and lay down the ideal conditions for such a union. First, he will have to remember that his different bodies reach maturity at different ages. The physical body is complete in all its parts at birth ; the desire-body does not come into function till puberty, which, indeed, marks the completion of the desire-body ; the tender affections develop during the teens, and the concrete mental body during the twenties. A strict septenary reckoning is employed by some schools of esoteric science, but individuals vary in their development, and the foregoing rough division will serve. The abstract mind develops during the thirties, and the spiritual nature will not have reached its full unfoldment till the late forties. Therefore the highly evolved individual should delay his mating till well on in life, when it can be seen which way his evolution is trending.

Many people, unfortunately, are hurried into a permanent mating by the activities of the desire-body, and resort to marriage with the first available person of the opposite sex as the only means of obtaining relief from gnawing desires. Other hasty people mistake emotional surging for the rapport of true union, not yet realising the capacities of their own nature, which may continue to develop after marriage. Well is it for a married pair if their growth be even and simultaneous. They will find in married life the deepening and enriching of their love as body after body comes into function and meets its mate within the home that is reaching up to heaven. If, on the contrary, one has reached full stature while the other is still capable of growth, the marriage which started happily will end in compromise or failure, since the more highly evolved of the two will be conscious of needs which the other cannot comprehend or satisfy.

In perfect marriage, however, the same pair mate with each higher body as it comes into function, experiencing with each mating new depths of love. Physical union in mutual desire will give harmony and poise to their nervous system ; love will blend desires and aims into one and bind the personalities together ; the acquisition of a common fund of knowledge will make companionship closer; belief in similar concepts and principles direct their lives into the same channel ; spiritual aims and ideals of the same order complete their union ; until, consciousness having risen to the level of pure spirit, this great love engendered between two souls will overflow all limitations and draw the whole universe into the bounds of their union. When this is achieved, it is held by the esoteric philosophers that the greatest stimulus which it is possible to give from the physical plane is applied to evolution. These two, thus mated upon all planes, " enter into the light and go not forth again " as separate individuals, but become one individual with a two-sided nature, complete in itself and self-fulfilling. Such beings, however, have passed to a higher order of life than ours and are uncognisable by our senses.

CHAPTER XVI

THE LAWS OF MATING UPON EACH PLANE

MATING upon each plane depends upon actual continuity of the substance of that plane; thus, upon the physical plane, union depends upon the interlocking of the generative organs and the injection of the male secretion into the female receptacle.

Upon the second plane mating is held to have taken place when desire is mutually inflamed, and a man " looketh upon a woman to lust after her " and she experiences a similar passion towards him.

Upon the third plane union depends upon emotional sympathy, and on the fourth plane on a common content of consciousness and interest.

On the fifth plane intellectual sympathy determines the mating, and on the sixth plane mutual spiritual ideals.

On the seventh plane All are One and One is All, no closer union being possible than that which has existed from the dawn of manifestation.

A peculiarity of this composite mating will be found in the fact that upon certain planes like mates with like, and upon others opposites are attracted to each other; in the first case the units augment each other, and in the other they supplement each other.

Upon the first plane opposites are drawn together, each being attracted by the difference in the body of the other. Upon the second plane attraction depends upon a mutual rousing of a similar passion, and there like attracts like. Upon the third plane difference again makes the attraction, those who have great powers of love being drawn towards those who need affection; there the protective instinct demands a mate that shall lean and make demands upon tenderness, while those who seek the comfort of love need the compassion and protection of their mate.

Upon the plane of the concrete mind a similar content of consciousness makes for sympathy, thus those who are interested in the same subjects find much in common; whereas upon the plane of the abstract mind those who approach their intellectual problems by different roads make the best mates, the critical counterchecking the imaginative, and the deductive illuminating the inductive.

Upon the sixth plane mating depends upon ray-colour, those of similar spiritual type mating with souls akin to themselves, and union being impossible between those of divergent rays.

Now it is said in esoteric science that mating upon each plane depends upon actual function, and individuals are said to be mated only so long as they are functioning in polarity; when the rapport ceases, mating ceases. Mating, therefore, must not be confused with marriage, which is a legal contract and depends for its validity upon the laws of equity and not upon actual function. Marriage is a contract entered into between the man and woman on the one part and the child on the other, and will be dealt with in a separate chapter ; this concept of marriage is only mentioned here in order to make clear the difference between marriage and mating as understood by the esotericist.

Mating upon the physical plane endures only for the few moments of coitus ; it can take place with any member of the opposite sex within the limits of the species.

Upon the second plane mating continues as long as desire continues—that is to say, only during the breeding-season or those years in the human being during which desire is active.

Third plane bodies are mated as long as there is affection.

Should the fourth plane body, with its content of consciousness built up during an incarnation, become mated, that mating will continue for the whole of the incarnation, and nothing but death can annul it.

When, however, mating extends up to the fifth plane between people of like ideals and principles, it has come into the sphere of the individuality which endures for an evolution, and for the remainder of that evolution will the bond continue, the souls waiting for each other and finding each other in life after life, and making that wonderful tie which, when once formed, will bring them together from the ends of the earth and break all other chains.

When union is confirmed on the spiritual plane, then the pair become one in actual fact and substance, and " entering the Light, return not again."

It will thus be seen that the esotericist's concept of mating is very different to the popular one. He declares mating to be a matter of actual function, and to cease when the function ceases. On the other hand, should mating extend to the physical plane, then there is always the possibility of offspring from the union to be considered, and to bring into the world a child for whom there is no home is to do that child a cruel wrong.

The Church, guided in many cases by men who had a profound illumination, knew that when a true spiritual union took place the bond was unbreakable and of a sacramental nature, and held up this ideal as the standard of Christian marriage. The teachings of the Church are truly applicable to a mating of individualities and rightly describe its conditions, but what shall be said concerning a union in which only the lower levels of the personality are concerned ?   This is in no wise a sacramental union, but simply a satisfaction of a physical need and instinctive desire, and should be considered from the standpoint of hygiene rather than theology.

The Church, guided nowadays by men who are further removed than the Early Fathers from the source of inspiration, makes no distinction between the two types of union, but applies the highest ideals indiscriminately, giving a sacramental blessing to that which is of no loftier a type than the conjugation of animals, and demanding of mortal clay that which only the spirit can afford. Were the Church more sparing of her blessing and less exacting in her standards, especially towards those not of her fold, we should be spared much social confusion.

No one knows better than the esotericist the indissoluble nature of a sacramental union, but he maintains that such a union can only take place between individualities which endure for an evolution. In this respect he goes even farther than the Churchman, holding that such a union is not even broken by death. The attitude of the Churchman is illogical in this matter, for if two beings are sacramentally united, then, if those beings are immortal, their union must endure throughout their immortality, and the death of the body of one party would not affect the bond.

The truth of the matter, as conceived by the esotericist, is that the union of individualities is sacramental and indissoluble, but that the union of personalities, or any level of them, continues only so long as function continues. The fact, however, that such union produces the vehicles needed for reincarnating souls complicates the whole issue, which otherwise was simple enough ; the rights of the children cut across the rights of the parents, and, from the point of view of the race, are paramount.

CHAPTER XVII

THE ESOTERIC TEACHING CONCERNING "TWIN SOULS"

It is well known to all observers of human nature that certain people seem to " bring out the best in each other," that, when they are together, each nature seems to blossom and to become capable of greater heights of development than could be reached alone, and at the same time a wonderful joy and radiance pervades them. Should they be parted from each other they droop and wither, and though time serves to alleviate the bitterness of severance, neither soul rises to its full stature in solitude. There may be no mournful and self-pitying brooding over the past, no morbid refusal to transfer interest to fresh objects, but there is an abiding sense of life lived below its normal level.

Such people may even fancy that they are not two separate entities, but the halves of a single whole. The close sympathy and perfect rapport between two such minds causes every mood to find its reflection in the other, so that the grief of one will plunge both in sorrow, and joy rejoice them equally.

Popular thought is well aware of these conditions, and the hope of their attainment is hidden in every heart ; however much experience may teach the unlikelihood of its realisation, yet the hope ever springs up anew, so deep-rooted among the instincts is it ; but though the hope is universal its realisation is rare, for a complete union with another demands complete abnegation of self, and souls capable of such selflessness are few. For such a union two equally selfless souls must join, it is not enough that one should give completely and the other merely receive. It is not even enough that each should give his or her all, each must give what the other needs, otherwise the sacrifice is unavailing, and herein lies the key to many of the problems of unrequited love.

A good comradeship is the best that most men and women can expect after the heat of passion has cooled with familiarity and the lessening of physical beauty ; and though such a comradeship is one of the noblest and most beautiful things on earth, yet it is not that closer mating to which we refer, and popular thought is well aware of this and has designated such mates as " twin souls," knowing that the bond far surpasses that which is known as married love, beautiful and profound as it is. The close and lifelong bond of married love, for whose fire the passion of lovers is but the kindling, is built of a thousand mutual needs, tendernesses, memories and sympathies arising out of companionship ; this other love knows no building, but is born full-grown and transcends all other ties, or, should the ties be maintained, breaks the soul.

Such a strong bond, that springs into being mature, cannot be regarded as a new birth, it is rather the reincarnation of a passion that was developed in past lives; though the conscious mind is ignorant, the subconscious remembers and claims its mate.

The phenomenon of this love in physical being is exceedingly rare, though commonplace passion or sudden emotional sympathy are easily exaggerated by their hungry souls into something higher than their reality. Individuals of a lowly evolution, and these are most liable to sudden and uncontrollable passions, are too egocentric, too bound up within their own limitations and appetites, to be capable of a lasting and harmonious union with any creature; still less can they realise the ideal of complete selflessness and service which is implied in the concept of another who shall be as one's very self. They have but little to bestow in return for the satisfaction of their hungry desires, and the one who undertakes to minister to these soon grows weary of the unrequited task.

The great majority of people are capable of a perfectly harmonious and satisfactory union with any member of a given type, or, in the language of esoteric science, with anyone who is upon the same ray as themselves. As was remarked in a previous chapter, spiritual mating can only take place between those who are of the same ray-colour, but whenever we meet one of our own ray there is a sense of fundamental harmony because the line of evolution and the spiritual qualities are the same, whether these qualities be highly developed or rudimentary. It is only upon fundamental harmony that a lasting and satisfying union can be built; it is useless to expect that development shall strengthen a tie when that very development is taking place in different directions. If a man should devote his life to a military career and attain eminence therein, it would be unlikely to draw him nearer to his wife if she had devoted hers to the cause of peace between nations.

Any person who is sufficiently evolved to be able to conceive an ideal and strive towards it must have regard to the ray-colour (denoted by the type of idealism) in choosing a mate, though the low types, who have no idea beyond self-interest, can mate on a basis of mutual passion and physical attraction and find as much satisfaction as they are capable of deriving from a union.

It may be stated that although esoteric science recognises the existence of " twin souls," it does not hold that every case of sudden and violent passion between individuals is such an indissoluble union ; it may be just what its name implies, passion and nothing more, dying down as quickly as it has sprung up and capable of renewal at the stimulus of a fresh object. Neither would esoteric science teach that the meeting of " twin souls," even if the supposed tie actually existed between them, was justification for any failure to discharge existing obligations ; though our divorce laws may have little relation to either the facts of human life or cosmic law, to break them incurs the penalties of society, and to inflict hardship upon an innocent person is no part of the Path of Enlightenment. Rather the esotericist would hold that as a single life is but a stage upon the soul's journey through evolution, we do best to sacrifice one short day of our existence in the honourable fulfilment of a bargain, so that future lives may be free from past debts and the great love harmoniously attained.

CHAPTER XVIII

THE NATURE OF THE TIES BETWEEN SOULS

(a) *The Karmic Tie*

ESOTERIC science recognises two types of tie that can draw souls together and bind them in a common fate. These binding ties, which originate upon the inner planes where the unseen causes operate, must be carefully distinguished from mutual attractions that arise upon the plane of effects, cognised by the physical senses.

The commonest type of bond is known as the Karmic Tie. The term Karmic (adjective of Karma) is borrowed from the Eastern Esoteric School, and is used, for convenience sake, to denote the forces, both good and bad, set going in previous incarnations. No corresponding English term exists ; the word Fate, its nearest equivalent, having come to mean, especially in its adjectival form, a force exclusively evil.

The Karmic Tie between souls has its root in attractions experienced in past lives. Attraction may occur upon any of the six planes of individualised existence and be of a nature appropriate to that plane. The attractions exercised upon the first or physical plane are simply a matter of physics. Gravitation, capillary attraction, absorption, and similar processes, take place upon the subplanes of dense matter; and magnetic attraction, chemical affinities, etc., manifest upon the etheric subplanes of our world. Emotional attraction does not exist below the second plane, where it makes itself felt in the urge of the instincts, therefore no tie is formed by mere physical propinquity; and emotional action and reaction have to occur before any bond is established.

It is reaction which is the essence of the bond. The fact that one person feels an emotion towards another does not link them together. It is only when the object of the emotion reacts towards it that a bond is formed, because he has then, as it were, taken into his own nature the force proceeding from the other and so formed a continuity of substance, however ethereal, and it is by means of this imperceptible thread that much of the work of practical occultism, both black and white, is performed.

Should one person love another and the love be reciprocated, a bond is formed; should one person love another and the love be returned by hate, contempt, loathing, or any form of resentment or unkindness, a bond will also be formed, and for the rest of their incarnation these rapports will influence the lives of those whom they unite in degrees proportionate to the intensity of the emotions that are experienced. It is only complete indifference that prevents a tie from being contracted, any emotional reaction sets up a rapport.

An action and its answering reaction upon any plane set up a rapport, whether the instincts be roused upon the second plane or the emotions on the third, the relationship of teacher and pupil or fellow-student upon the planes of the mind, or of priest, spiritual guide, or fellow-worshipper on the sixth plane. Upon whatever plane an action and reaction take place a bond is formed between the two interacting units.

These bonds may set up the most intimate relationship, or be a momentary contact immediately forgotten by those concerned, but as long as any emotion in relation to the memory exists the rapport will remain. Should emotion towards a particular person still be felt at the time of death, this emotion, having no means of gratification in the subjective state that follows on death, is stored up until, objective existence having been resumed in a new incarnation, the conditions for its expression are again available. *It is this unexhausted emotion which forms the Karmic Tie ;* and though it waits for hundreds of years, as time is reckoned in revolutions of the earth, it loses none of its force, but reacts to the same objects that previously stimulated it whenever those objects shall again become present. Hence the sudden outrush of " love at first sight " and the sense of understanding and intimacy which " twin souls " experience.

Each renewal of a Karmic Tie increases its strength, and though it may start as the merest carnal attraction in the childhood of the race, as body after body comes into function in the course of evolution, the rapport will spread from one to another until a great spiritual mating be achieved. If, however, the bodies of the pair fail to develop synchronously, then a strong bond will exist upon the lower planes, and the higher self of the more advanced individual be left unmated and unsatisfied, possibly loathing the response of its own lower nature to a degrading attraction, yet unable to free itself therefrom. Such a predicament threatens danger and suffering and frequently causes those tragedies of passion and crime that in all periods of history bear witness to the primitive forces that civilisation seeks to control.

A Karmic Tie, however, only develops great strength when all the forces of the nature are concentrated upon a single object with great intensity of feeling; this happens comparatively rarely, unless the desires are thwarted under tragic conditions. A consummated passion usually sleeps the sleep of repletion; but should those who love be parted, either by circumstances or by death, then the unfulfilled love remains as a bond upon the third plane, which for a long time is unaffected by the death of the body. If the parting be by death, and if the survivor, either in sleep, as often happens, or by means of psychic development, become conscious, even momentarily, of the third plane of existence, the bond that exists thereon will draw the two souls into contact again. This is the true means of communication with the departed, to exalt consciousness so that we become aware of their state of existence, not to recall them to awareness of our mundane condition by means of a medium. . . . A medium should only be resorted to in the case of a soul that is earthbound and cannot proceed to its own sphere, and then only for the purpose of giving it quittance.

The third plane is the sphere of existence referred to in spiritualistic literature as the heaven-world ; but before the out-going soul, released from its body, can attain to this state, it has to pass through a phase of second-plane existence known as purgatory, where arrears of evil are paid off in the suffering brought about by subjective realisation, thereby adjusting balance of fate. Once the soul is released from the deadening influences of the physical body all subtle forces become increasingly tangible, and although the newcomer cannot transcend his own plane of existence till his debts be worked out, the soul that has gone on ahead may, if sufficiently evolved, make telepathic contact with him for short periods, and so give help and comfort upon the hardest part of death's journey. As soon as the soul of the newcomer has risen above its purgatorial experience it enters the " heaven-world," and is then upon approximately the same plane as its mate. No barrier of differing states of existence now keeps them apart, the bond of love exerting its natural attraction draws them together ; they can then pass the rest of their time between incarnations in companionship. The bond between them will tend to draw them into incarnation again at the same time and under similar conditions, and then upon meeting will come that strange uprush of sub-conscious memory so incomprehensible to those whose philosophy does not extend beyond a single life on a single plane, but so readily explicable in terms of the esoteric doctrines.

Should two souls be drawn together life after life by these means, in each life loving and companion-ing each other and steadfastly eschewing all other attractions, the bond thus formed will become very strong. This, however, but rarely happens. It does not require many incarnations, with the long discarnate periods that intervene between them, to take us back to the ages when human civilisation was in its infancy and nothing loftier than second plane unions were being formed. As is well known, low-level unions are formed with great facility and are of little endurance, so that a soul, even in the course of a single incarnation, may have formed several ties of this nature, especially in civilisations where polygamy was practised. Each of such unions will be able to exercise a drawing power in pro-portion to its intensity upon the plane on which it took place, so that the soul that has contracted such unions, and few have not, will be pulled in different directions by the ties it has formed.

Let us consider the progress of a soul through

evolution, sometimes in a male body, sometimes in
a female. In the earliest phases of human evolution
union took place simply in response to the promptings of instinct, as it does now among animals;
thus only two bodies were involved, the physical
body, by means of which the union was carried out,
and the desire-body of the second plane, which
prompted the union. A first plane union can take
place with any member of the opposite sex of the
same species that has attained a sufficient age, and
such a union, involving no emotions, leaves no
trace. Second plane unions depend upon the
arousing of mutual passion, and such an experience modifies the soul to this extent—that it will
readily experience a recrudescence of its passion
when it again meets an individual that has once
shared in its excitement. This accounts for those
amazing intoxications of the senses which sometimes
lure men and women into experiences that leave
bitter regrets behind.

But although these second plane attractions can
cause a wild ebullition of passion which it requires
considerable force of character to master, they are
usually short-lived; it is not until a soul has evolved
sufficiently to be capable of a third plane union that
a bond is formed which extends beyond the senses
and is capable of influencing character. Even here
several unions can be formed in a single incarnation.
Esoteric science does not teach that souls are created
as twins, but that such unions are built in the course
of many incarnations; and it will be seen from the

preceding paragraphs that many vicissitudes may befall the soul while it is still at a primitive and unevolved stage of development, and these fleeting unions entered into at the bidding of the instincts, the only mentors that primitive types recognise, militate one against another and prevent any lasting union being formed, for it is only by the fidelity of many lives that the union known as " twin souls " can be achieved.

Should, however, two souls be so strongly drawn together that each has the power to hold the other against all comers, then (provided they are not too dissimilar in type), as body by body comes into function in the course of evolution, they will mate upon the higher planes, and that wonderful union of perfect sympathy and understanding, so beautiful and so rarely seen, will be achieved. Should, however, the pair be of different spiritual type, then tragedy will occur as the higher natures come into function and draw them apart at the bidding of a different idealism. Ancient faiths, such as the Catholic and the Jewish, with their roots deep in the esoteric lore of the past, know this, and there-fore forbid intermarriage with those of another communion.

It will be seen from the foregoing pages wherein lies the danger of light and promiscuous relations popularly referred to as the sowing of wild oats. Such unions set up a rapport that is easier formed than broken, and lay snares for the soul in future lives. Among primitive peoples, who have much knowledge of practical occultism, a great deal of attention is given to sex-magic, one of the most potent forms of magic that exists, and in many parts of the world there is considerable traditional knowledge of genuine occult methods in addition to an acquaintance with aphrodisiac drugs ; and the men of a higher civilisation, who abuse their power in reference to women of primitive tribes, sometimes find that they have involved themselves in a bond that is not easily broken, and contacted forces whose subtlety is only equalled by their unpleasantness.

(b) *The Cosmic Tie*

There is an aspect of the sex-relationship even less understood than that which has been outlined in the foregoing chapter. The bond between souls which is known to esotericists as the Cosmic Tie is one of the most profound and potent, and at the same time most beautiful, of the secrets of the Western Esoteric Tradition. European civilisation has always valued women highly, holding that if one-half of the citizens of a country is in a retrograde state the standard of evolution for the whole race must be lowered. The general attitude of the white races is reflected in their esoteric tradition, wherein it is held that souls, while incarnated in the negative or feminine vehicle, have not only got special lessons to learn, but also special potencies, and the greatest importance is attached to the co-operation of male and female forces in any work involving practical occultism. In certain orders it is the custom to keep the lodge-membership evenly balanced between the sexes, and not to allow the predominance of either sex to go beyond a certain proportion.

Taking electricity as a type of force closely analogous to the invisible potencies which underlie the visible world and determine its conditions, the occultist knows that every force must have, not only an outflowing from the Divine, but also a Path of Returning; also that any form which acts as a transmitter of such force must have a positive and negative aspect. The male vehicle is positive and the female negative, and therefore the practical occultist finds that for certain types of work it is necessary to function in partnership or polarity, for only thus can a circuit be set up and a flow of cosmic force be induced.

As has been explained in a previous chapter, the vehicles corresponding to the different planes are positive and negative in relation to each other. The individuality is positive in relation to the person- ality, which is negative towards the higher potency of its greater self. If an individual is sufficiently evolved to have any of the levels of his individuality in function and fully correlated with his conscious- ness, he can cause the flow and return of cosmic force to take place within his own organism, and thereby attain a considerable degree of power and enlightenment. For instance, the spiritual ideals and aims, and the abstract perceptions of principles belonging to the fifth and sixth vehicles can be used to illumine and inspire the activities of the personality.

On the other hand, for the use of the greater potencies and the operations of the higher occultism, it is necessary to have a pair working in polarity; only so can the great cosmic voltages be carried without the danger of " earthing," so well known to all practical occultists. The pair, working thus, open a channel for the Divine forces which flow through them with astounding power, and magnetise not only themselves but their immediate neighbourhood. By this means the powers of each are tremendously augmented, and the whole nature is vivified and brought to the highest perfection of its capacities. If the greater cosmic forces should be called down by an individual who is not working in conjunction with another who is a suitable channel of return, they will be very apt to make a path of returning for themselves through any conductile vehicle that approaches sufficiently close, leaping the gap like an electric spark; and if the individual who receives the force be of insufficient calibre to carry the voltage, her emotional nature will, metaphorically speaking, fuse, and there will be an open circuit of cosmic forces which will also fuse the positive or male vehicle, burn all in their immediate neighbourhood, and break the contact with the Divine forces. Anyone who is familiar with those circles that are interested in occult studies must have seen this happen, for it is a very common occurrence among those who, while only partially instructed, seek to operate the unseen forces.   How often does some man, who as a teacher and initiator is doing fine work, suddenly cast all aside for the sake of a woman who, utterly unworthy of him, drags him down from the high calling whereunto he was called ; this is so common an occurrence that those who have knowledge are most cautious, and rightly so, ere enrolling themselves as pupils under outstanding personalities, however great may be the benefits to be derived from so doing, for the blowing of a fuse on the physical plane is as nothing to what happens when an analogous accident happens in occult work.

If these forces be rightly understood and employed, however, the highest occult work can be done in safety ; it is because the perfect circuit is not always available that the handling of certain potencies becomes a dangerous task ; devices of the nature of lightning-conductors have to be employed, and they are not always perfectly satisfactory.   It must not be thought that occultists dwell intemperately upon the subject of sex, or that they are more sensual than their fellow-men who follow other lines of study, but, as their researches are into the very foundations of human nature, they must take the sexual forces into their calculations, or else they would run the risk of being caught unawares by the tides they have ignored.   Occultists deal with the forces of life itself, and one aspect of life-force is certainly sex-force.   As has been shown

in a previous chapter, the life-forces run down
through all the seven bodies of man as pure force,
and are conditioned by the nature of the body,
mental, emotional, or physical, as the case may be,
through which they take form. Life itself is not
thought any more than it is sperm; but if it is
used to drive the machinery of the mental body it
will produce thought, and if it is turned into the
machinery of the reproductive organs it will produce sperm. It will, in fact, go to whatever part
of our nature we direct our attention, and if we have
not trained ourselves sufficiently in thought-control
to be sure of keeping our minds off any particular
subject for a certain period, we are running
grave risks if we open the channels of our nature
to more force than it is normally constructed to
deal with. This risky enlargement of receptiveness
is effected by certain forms of breathing, meditation,
or ritual magic, and the risk lies in the fact that if a
sensual thought intrude into consciousness at a
time when the channels are open and the forces are
flowing, those forces will immediately follow the
focus of attention, and the result will be an outbreak of passion and sensuality. It is by concentration of thought that these powers are held to
their work, just as the automobile is steered by the
driver's hands. If attention waver, the direction
of the power will waver with it. To use a big occult
potency is like driving a high-powered car at a high
speed, all depends on the control; unless you have
the nerve for it, you are safer on your feet. Many

people experiment in the invocation of forces, but few are aware of their reality until they find themselves out of their depth.

The rightly trained occultist, knowing these facts, will refrain, then, from certain kinds of work if he is unable to obtain a complete circuit for the cosmic force. It was said to the writer once, " Only those who are rightly married can go to the higher degrees." The most important work is done by the pair, not by the solitary worker, who is always more or less unstable, and nothing in occultism is more undesirable than instability. For such work the closest sympathetic rapport of the higher nature is necessary, and such intimacy and propinquity is only sanctioned by our society when it has been regularised by marriage. Union upon the physical plane need not take place, and, in fact, will not take place while the life-forces are being used upon other levels ; but when that work is not going on, and few have the stamina to keep it up continuously and without respite, then the forces will tend to follow their natural channel, and if that channel is not open, trouble may ensue. Moreover, should certain of the operations of practical magic not be entirely successful, then it is very advantageous to be able to run the unutilised forces off through the ordinary channels of nature upon the physical plane. It is possible for a man and a woman to work together for a life-time without having recourse to the physical plane, but it is only highly evolved and disciplined natures that are capable of such restraint, and people who undertake a partnership that cannot, if necessary, be placed upon the basis of legal marriage, should realise that they have set themselves no light task.

It may be deemed unjust that anyone should be delayed in their spiritual progress because circumstances have denied them a suitable partner; this, however, is not the case when envisaged from the point of view of the occultist. If the student has advanced far enough to undertake the operations indicated in the foregoing pages, he will be an initiate of the greater mysteries, and will have shifted the focus of his life from the personality to the individuality; he will have some memory of past incarnations, realise that they are phases of his existence, and his sense of the " I " will stretch beyond both birth and death. He will know that the circumstances of his present life depend upon conditions in past lives, just as the circumstances of our old age depend upon the actions of our youth and manhood. He will see a future of many lives stretching out before him, and he will know that that future is under his control; therefore he does not feel that he must taste or forego any particular experience altogether before death shall overtake him; certain work he may decide to set aside for another incarnation, seeing that the conditions of this one are unsuitable for its execution. The fact that he feels an urge to mate does not necessarily mean that he is ready for the great cosmic mating which we are here contemplating. Such a union requires more than his own decision; but should he have come to the point when he must handle *focussed* cosmic forces, then for this purpose he will have to effect the cosmic mating, which is a mating, not of personal love, but of capacity for service along the same lines of power. No love may enter into the union at the outset; indeed, it may be a union of complete strangers, although out of the deep harmony necessary for the formation of a circuit, love may grow.

The Cosmic Tie is a union that is entered into by two individuals for the purpose of performing certain occult work that can only be carried out by two units functioning in polarity; it has nothing whatever to do with love or attraction as ordinarily understood. It is motived by service and nothing else; it is partnership entered into for the sake of the work to be performed. The participants in this union do not choose their partners, they offer themselves for service to the Master on the inner planes, whose pupils they are; and by the Wisdom of a higher plane they are mated with regard to their qualities and capacities for service according to ray-colour.

The essential difference between the Karmic and the Cosmic Tie lies in the fact that the Karmic Tie begins upon the lowest plane and works upwards as body after body comes into function; whereas the Cosmic Tie begins upon the highest plane and works downwards. The Karmic Tie is part of the normal discipline of evolution; the Cosmic Tie is supernormal in that it belongs to a different code of laws altogether to that which governs the general order of mankind ; it is one of the Greater Mysteries, and, as such, is reserved for initiates, and is only referred to here because so many are essaying these mysteries without initiation—are experimenting with great natural forces in entire ignorance of their nature and potency, and therein lies danger.

CHAPTER XIX

HOW SOULS FIND THEIR MATES

First Section

SOULS can achieve mating in three different ways: firstly, through the ordinary attractions of sex; secondly, by the renewing of Karmic Ties; and thirdly, according to the higher Cosmic Laws. Each of these forms of attraction needs to be understood if we are to adjust our lives truly and harmoniously, for each of us may be drawn to another in all three ways; and we must not forget that as long as we are human at all we shall have capacity for response to the lure of sex, a capacity which needs to be qualified by the guidance of the reason lest it prove a dangerous and short-sighted guide.

The readiness of our response to the lure of sex is due to the rise and fall of certain physiological tides within the organism, and we must always remind ourselves that the appeal a certain person makes to our emotions may simply be due to the fact that we are in an emotional state; broadly speaking, after the age of puberty has been reached, a member of the opposite sex will attract us unless that person has attributes whose repulsiveness suffices to counterbalance the fascination; discrepancies of age, social status, or physical defects neutralise the instinctive attraction, unless that attraction is exceptionally strong.

Should there be no immediate barrier, however, and mating take place in response to a physical urge translated as emotion, then the success of that mating will depend upon the harmony or disharmony revealed by experience between the two characters. A union entered into without reflection is as much dependent upon luck for its happiness as is the turning up of double sixes in a throw of dice—and as rare.

Such unions are surprisingly common, even among those who would be reckoned as educated and enlightened. Young people, feeling the unaccustomed pressure of the sex-tides steadily rising within them, marry as soon as their finances permit, and even sooner, in order to escape from the emotional stresses to which they are subjected, and to make their appetites fit in with their ideals. They erroneously "rationalise" their feelings and amazingly idealise the object of them, with the result that their physical needs being satisfied and rendered quiescent, they wake up to find themselves bound for life to a person who is incapable of satisfying any of their other needs of mind, heart, or spirit. Misery follows; taught by experience, they learn too late the requirements of harmonious mating. We have only to look around us to see how often a second marriage is a happy one; but, unfortunately, our laws denying the opportunity of a second marriage unless death or public divorce terminate the first, men and women live on in a union which has failed of its purpose, or enter into an arrangement upon which society's disapproval weighs so heavily that it seldom fulfils its purpose either.

But though the vast majority of us marry in obedience to Nature's simplest laws, the laws under whose sway are the flowers of the field and the beasts that perish, but which are, none the less, divine laws and not to be despised, let us also realise that matings of higher types are governed by higher laws, obedience to which will ensure harmony.

People who have read esoteric literature, and have realised that there are other bonds between souls than those of sexual attraction, may be tempted to despise these simple but most potent forces, and to refuse a union which they fear may be commonplace for the sake of some destined Karmic mate to whom they have been bound in past lives, and whose coming they await. Herein lies one of the dangers of the divulgence of secret occult doctrines. Had such an one known nothing of occultism he might have made a happy union according to Nature's laws; but, knowing enough to reject the guidance of his instincts, and insufficient to differentiate between fantasies arising from subconscious wishes and the promptings of the individuality, he may throw away the lower without gaining the higher. The trained occultist knows how to counter-check these things, the seeker does not. The methods of counter-checking psychism cannot be given here. The reader is advised to make an earnest self-examination before staking his own and another person's happiness on an unverified impulse which may be unreasonable.

Under such circumstances he should test and counter-check his impulse as carefully as lies in his power. First, he should allow himself ample time to discover whether his intuitive feeling that there is some soul to whom he is bound by Karmic ties strengthens or weakens with the passage of months, or even years. Secondly, if there is a destined mate awaiting him, any reliable psychic ought to be able to discern the fact and confirm his impression. Psychics, however, are no more infallible than doctors, especially such psychics as make a business matter of a sacred power, and whoever makes use of their services would do well to consult at least three, and see if their readings tally with one another. In addition to this, an astrologer provided with data for a horoscope will be able to tell almost the exact date when the fateful meeting will take place. Unless the reports of the psychics confirm each other, and astrologers, casting horoscopes independently, agree as to date, the would-be explorer of the unseen would be wise to regard the promptings of his intuition as indications of the needs of his own nature as translated by the fantasies of his subconscious mind, and to wait until the call to initiation comes, as come it will when he is ripe, before seeking to explore the unseen without a guide, and run the risks involved in so doing.

A well-known writer, discoursing upon love and marriage and casting ridicule upon the idea that any tie beyond instinctive attraction could exist between men and women, pointed out that it was a curious coincidence that soul-mates should be born in the same neighbourhood, or, out of the whole huge world, meet each other when the mating time comes. Esoteric science teaches, however, that agencies are actually at work to bring about these meetings, just as similar agencies govern the migrations of the birds and the return of the comets. It is, of course, well known that the date of a comet's return can be confidently predicted by the mathematics of astronomy. With regard to the meetings of " soul-mates," they are regulated by the workings of the force popularly known as karma, or destiny, the sum-total of the causes set going in the past which determine the conditions of the present ; into the details of these laws it is impossible to enter in these pages ; it must suffice to say that, after death, souls gather into themselves the fruits of the experiences of the life that is just finished, and when the time comes for them to incarnate again, they are sent into incarnation through the agency of certain forces at the moment when the planetary influences give the conditions for the working out of the appointed fate. Therefore, an astrologer who knows the exact moment of birth can, by a study of the horoscope, tell what karma has to be worked out in the course of the incarnation and also the exact dates when the crises will occur. These secret laws form an important part of the studies of occult science, and by means of a knowledge of their workings predictions can be made with considerable accuracy. The details of their workings are too complex for consideration in these pages, and it must suffice to say, concerning the nature of the karmic tie between souls, that it will act as the tides of the sea : and only the greatest of adepts can influence its effects. We cannot control the results of the causes we have set going in past lives, though we can control our reactions to the conditions they bring to us. It is only in the future that we can find full scope for our will, for in the ever-moving present we are setting in motion the causes that will meet us face to face when their circuit is completed.

Second Section

In knowledge of the laws of cosmic mating lies our best hope of deliverance from difficulties in which ignorance and false doctrines have involved the " marriage problem." In an earlier stage of evolution, man lived close to nature, knew less of free-will, memory, and reason, and was entirely guided by his instincts. When course of time brought the development of the higher mind, however, the problem was greatly complicated. Instinct was a sufficient guide when the mating of the lower planes of the personality alone were involved, but when the individuality with its relationship to evolution and the cosmos as a whole began to function and required mating for its full development and expression, instinct was no longer an adequate guide because factors had to be taken into consideration which were beyond the scope of the lower nature. Reason and spiritual intuition have to be employed for the direction of the greater self; we have to rise superior to the pain and pleasure of the moment, or even of the incarnation, and base our lives upon the universal and eternal if the greater life that looks beyond birth and death is to be fulfilled of its purpose.

Let us imagine the case of a man who, while capable of normal response to the call of sex, and having, as we all have, ties with the past, desires to be bound by none of these things, but to mate upon the highest plane that evolution has opened up for the functioning of our race. What must be his procedure? Upon the physical plane he will remain entirely passive, neither seeking nor avoiding any contact that might bring to him his mate; upon the lower astral plane he will call home the passions, and try so to sublimate them by abstemious living and thought-control that they shall not be insistent, for it is not by the light of the passions that a mate can be chosen according to the higher laws. Upon the third plane of

the tender affections he should let love flow out
to all things so that, by whatever path the mate
may come, she may be met by love and drawn
within the gate. Then he should raise his consciousness to the highest plane upon which he
is capable of functioning by meditating upon the
loftiest ideals that he can conceive, and, with
consciousness elevated to this state, he should
dwell upon the characteristics of the mate who
would satisfy his needs. Having dwelt upon these
characteristics till a well-defined image is built up
in his mind, he may then imagine himself seeking
and calling, making himself heard by the very
insistence of his endeavour, until a soul, whose
nature shall have placed it upon the plane to which
he has lifted himself by meditation, shall hear the
call and respond.

When such a union has been effected upon the
inner planes, its effects become visible in the inner
life long before any meeting takes place upon the
plane of manifestation; the peace of true mating
comes upon the soul though no mate has as yet
appeared in the world of sense. Sometimes the
meeting never takes place upon the physical plane,
karmic conditions forbidding, but the rapport
remains and can be developed and yield all that the
higher nature requires. Indeed, a mate may be
found who has passed the phase of evolution
during which incarnation takes place, and that
strange partnership between the unseen and the
seen may be built up. It is by such a partnership

that much of the work of the Masters is carried on. These things can be no more than hinted at ; those who are sufficiently evolved to experience them are sufficiently evolved to obtain the guidance they need. Again, warning must be given against mistaking subjective phantasy for objective fact ; our safest guide in these matters is humility, which does not imagine great things of itself, but seeks to serve in all ways that lie to hand and accepts gratefully what each day brings. To the humble and kind the great experiences come, rather than to those who are urged on by curiosity and ungratified vanity. People who cannot deal with life successfully upon a single plane of existence are ill-advised to multiply their difficulties by expanding their consciousness.

CHAPTER XX

ESOTERIC TEACHING CONCERNING MARRIAGE

ONE of the chief causes of the problems surrounding marriage in modern life is the convention which prevents us from honestly facing the facts with which we have to deal. The esoteric scientist, whose aim it is to understand and control the causes behind appearances, has, by the very nature of his pursuit, to look facts in the face.

It will have been noticed that, in the preceding pages, much has been said concerning mating of souls, but the word " marriage " has seldom been used, and for this reason, that mating and marriage are in fact two different things. " Mating " means the functioning in polarity of two organisms so that, for the time being, they form the halves of a single whole ; marriage is a legal contract. Mating is an actual fact ; one is either mated or not mated, just as the electric light is turned either on or off ; but marriage is a fluctuating convention. Who would maintain that an English marriage, with the free and honoured status it accords to women, is the same thing as a Turkish marriage ? Yet both are according to the law of their respective lands.

And is an English marriage to-day the same as it was a hundred, or even fifty years ago ?

Marriage is a very great deal more than mating, it is a partnership in the business of life, and the marriage laws are society's attempt to standardise the treatment which the different members of the home are to receive from each other. Firstly, there are the duties of the husband and wife toward each other ; secondly, there are the obligations they undertake toward society through their children, and these duties and obligations have to be considered in the framing of marriage laws. Those marriage laws are the best which most closely approximate to a codification of natural laws. Unfortunately the laws of marriage in England are very far from approaching to the perfection possible to such instruments, but under these laws we have to live, and the needs of human nature are obliged to achieve a compromise with the demands of the State.

The esotericist considers the marriage laws and the keeping or breaking thereof from the point of view of karma ; it is his aim to set no forces in motion save those which are in harmony with the divine law. If the marriage laws of his country are at variance with natural law, and he abide by them, he will suffer from his disregard of natural law, but he will lay up for himself no causes potent for evil in the future. On the other hand, should he disregard the social code, though he may enhance his own comfort he will cause suffering to others, and that suffering, according to the laws of karma, will return upon his own head and delay his progress. Whether the marriage laws of a country are sound or not, we cannot get away from the fact that the marriage contract is a bargain, and that the breaker of promises forfeits his honour.

Should, however, one party to a bargain fail to meet his obligations, then, according to the laws of contract, the other party is released ; it is only in regard to the marriage contract that the law, instructed by theologians, retains the aggrieved person in bondage, and it is contrary to equity in so doing. The esotericist believes that failure to fulfil the obligations of marriage by one party leaves the other morally, if not legally, free—free, that is to say, from his obligations to his guilty partner, but not free to enter into unlegalised relations with a third person, because by so doing great suffering is caused by exposing that person to the rigours of the social code, and a terrible wrong may be done to a soul by causing it to incarnate under circumstances in which no proper home can be afforded to it. People have the right to sacrifice their own lives, but not those of others ; and the occultist, believing a soul to be no less alive and personalised because for the moment it is unattached to a physical body, takes an even more serious view of unchastity than does the world at large, but he regards it not so much as an offence against the person as a sin against the unborn. If there were any certain method of preventing conception then the matter would be upon a different footing, for the two adults concerned would affect no lives but their own; but the only certain method of preventing conception is to abstain from intercourse, and such abstention the laws of the higher life enjoin upon those who cannot legalise their union and its possible issue.

CHAPTER XXI

ESOTERIC ATTITUDE TOWARDS THE CHILD

ESOTERIC science does not regard each child born into the world as a newly created soul. Though the little body is newly made, the life that ensouls it was individualised many thousands of years ago, and the experiences through which that life has passed determine the character-traits of the new personality just as the causes set going in past lives determine the conditions into which it is reborn. If the parents make a good environment for the children they hope to have, souls of a high type can reincarnate through them. This, then, is the essence of the esotericist's concept of the relation of parent and child; the parents opened a channel whereby a soul can reincarnate and so advance in its evolution, and this deed stands to the credit of the parents in the great account of fate.

A point arises out of this concept which must be touched upon to render the concept clear, although it does not strictly concern the subject of esoteric sex. As each one of us affects the lives of those with whom we come in contact, bringing them good or evil, we are each agents of the fate that allots the dues earned in past existences. If we bring good to others we thereby, under the law of cause and effect, lay up good for ourselves that we shall reap in the next life if not in this one ; and if we do evil we shall likewise be repaid in our own coin. It may be argued that it is each person's fate that brings them good or evil, and therefore the agent of fate is not responsible for his actions towards them. The answer to this problem is, that though each person indeed draws towards himself the conditions that he has earned, one's merit may cause one to be the vehicle of the good he has earned and not of the evil. If one has laid up a store of evil causation, it may be one's punishment to be the channel through which the suffering has to come, and so pay compound interest on wrong-doing. " It must be that evil come, but woe unto him through whom it comes."

Even the best of parents may sometimes have to be the channel of suffering to their children through financial losses or unsuspected hereditary disease, but in order to get such happenings into their true perspective they must look at them from the stand-point of an evolution, not of a single incarnation, and train their children to make the best possible reaction to their environment, thus converting evil into good. It must also be remembered that suffering is not necessarily synonymous with evil, and that some valuable experiences only come through pain and trial.

Parents, however, should carefully refrain from the deliberate admission of souls into poverty-stricken homes, or of an enfeebled or diseased physique, thereby piling up further evil for themselves in the future; and out of this arises the vexed question of the prevention of conception, which will be dealt with later, after an explanation of the conditions of incarnation will have rendered possible an understanding of this subject from the esoteric point of view.

We will now consider what happens when a soul, having contemplated its sins in purgatory and its good deeds in a state equivalent to the ordinary concept of heaven, prepares to return once more to the earth in order to undergo further experience. Through the operation of certain great laws too complex for consideration here, that soul is brought to the time and place where the conditions of conception are about to occur under such circumstances that the body so made would come into an environment suitable for the working out of the fate due to the incarnating soul.

The spermatozoa having come into the neighbourhood of the ovum by the ordinary physical means, it is well known that fertilisation may or may not occur, and the laws governing this chance, apart from physical obstructions or defects in seed or egg, are unknown to exoteric science. Esoteric science, however, teaches that, should there be a soul ripe for incarnation under such circumstances, it would slip into the vehicle so provided and clinch the

8

matter. If there should be no such soul, however, or should the astrological conditions nine months ahead be unsuitable for the administration of its fate by means of planetary influences, the opportunity for birth will be rejected, and no ensouling life being available, that ovum will merely decay and be cast out in the ordinary course of nature.

When the act of sexual union takes place the subtle forces of the two natures rush together, and, as in the case of two currents of water in collision, a whirlpool or vortex is set up ; this vortex extends up the planes as far as the mating of the corresponding bodies takes place, so that should two people who idealise each other, and whose love has elements of a spiritual nature in its composition, meet in coitus, the vortex so created will extend on to one of the higher planes. If, however, two people whose concept of love is confined to physical pleasure set up a vortex of ingress, as it is called, their vortex will extend no higher then the second plane of the animal passions. Souls await incarnation upon the plane of the inner world appropriate to their state of consciousness, just as, immediately on passing out of incarnation, they " think themselves into their own place." It is by means of the vortex of ingress that souls are enabled to pass down the planes and make contact with a molecule of dense matter and so gain a foothold upon the plane of manifestation, for it is with this vitalised molecule as a nucleus that the body of dense matter is built up around them. It therefore follows that the higher the vortex of ingress extends up the planes, the loftier will be the type of soul which is drawn through it into incarnation, for a very different type of soul awaits its time upon the upper mental plane from that which finds its appropriate conditions upon the lower astral.

If two people wish to call into incarnation a soul that is worthy of the services they are prepared to render it as parents, and who, this boon having been granted, are prepared to stand aside selflessly so that that soul, having attained adulthood, may be free to serve the world unfettered by the bonds of a personal love drawn too close, then they should preface union by meditation upon the highest ideals they can conceive, and maintain this meditation throughout union without permitting the mind to drop to the experience of physical sensation to the exclusion of all other consciousness. Through the vortex thus opened souls of a very lofty character can come into incarnation, but parents must remember that souls so conceived will never " belong " to them in the way that children of a more personal union belong to the family into which they come ; swans make ugly ducklings, and the greater the soul that so incarnates the greater the demands it will make upon those who nurture it. Different standards, different ideals, different ways of life, and even different conditions of physical health, will make great demands upon the wisdom and forbearance of those who essay such a task. Together with the knowledge that makes these first steps in practical occultism available for the generality of mankind, the warning must be given that such an undertaking is no light burden, and that great qualities of mind and character are necessary for its successful completion. Should the character be uneven in its development, so that, although it can envisage great ideals, the lower nature is still strong enough to turn it from its course, then the discipline that will surround it will prove hard and exacting, for the lower will be sacrificed to the higher, the parent to the child, if there should be a conflict of interest between the two. If, however, the parents prove worthy of the trust reposed in them, they will find that the path from the higher planes whereby their child came to them stands open for their own advancement.

CHAPTER XXII

ESOTERIC TEACHING CONCERNING THE PREVENTION OF CONCEPTION AND ABORTION

THE esotericist regards life as a force whose nature is determined by the machinery through which it is brought into action, and he also holds that each plane has its own function to fulfil in the polity of the cosmos. Life, working through the generative organs upon the physical plane, has for its task the creation of vehicles for incoming souls, and should not, strictly speaking, be used for any other purpose ; if so used, it is wasted. On the other hand, if the life-force has been permitted to enter the first plane body in greater quantities than are necessary for the maintenance of that body, then it will cause serious trouble, both mental and physical, if it be not allowed to complete the circuit. In such a case, if it is undesirable that souls should be brought into incarnation under the circumstance, it is better to resort to the use of contraceptives than to submit to a repression of the life-forces which may affect both physical and mental health. But such a use must not be abused, it should be regarded rather as a medicinal measure, and not as a means of obtaining the pleasures of sexual intercourse without meeting its obligations. Those who, being in a position to provide incoming souls with sound physical bodies, selfishly refrain from doing so, sin against life itself, and their union is unhallowed though Church and State may have united to give it their blessing. No union receives the cosmic blessing until it has borne fruit, whether that fruit be of the body or of the spirit.

False concepts concerning sex-hygiene are of two types, those which declare constant sex-intercourse to be absolutely necessary and those which declare all sex intercourse to be absolutely unnecessary. Neither of these opinions are true. Life must flow in a circuit, and for so doing the positive and negative poles of manifestation are necessary, but the point of union need not be the physical generative organs, it may be the mind, or it may be the spirit. If we read a book by one of greater intellect than our own, we may be stimulated to creative activity, because his mind has fertilised ours ; herein we have an instance of polarity in the cosmic sense.

It will surprise many to learn that the benefits of sexual intercourse are derived, not from the physical reactions thereby brought about, but from the currents set up in the etheric doubles or counter-parts of subtle matter upon which the dense physical bodies are built up, and can be achieved by the blending of auras—those emanations of luminous mist which the psychic sees surrounding the human form. It may be asked, If this be so, then why do

we not enter into this relationship with the people
we sit next to in the bus or train ?   It is because lack
of sympathetic response prevents anyone from
penetrating the surface of the aura ; but where there
is sympathetic response, then aura blends with aura
until the two bodies are encased in a single auric
shell, and it is in this that the virtue of sex-intercourse lies—in the proximity, not in the orgasm ;
and, likewise, in the absence of such an interchange
of life-forces lies the harm of self-abuse.

The life-forces can be prevented from entering
upon the physical plane by building a channel for
them upon one of the subtler planes and causing
them to flow therein, but it is impossible to close
all the sluices and avoid undue pressure.   The life-
forces will always follow the focus of attention.   If
we concentrate upon the mental, they will flow to the
mind, and the physical body will remain quiescent ;
but if our thoughts dwell upon the generative organs,
the life-forces will very soon make their presence
felt therein.   Therefore, if we do not desire the life-
forces to flow through the channel of these organs,
we can effectually prevent their doing so by keeping
our thoughts away from that aspect of our nature ;
it is simply a question of thought-control, and whoso
has not attained to thought-control is ill-advised to
embark upon the pursuit of practical occultism.

Finally, to sum up the esoteric attitude towards
the prevention of conception—contraceptives are
better than nervous disease, but thought-control
and the direction of the life-forces into channels in

which they can do creative work rather than into one in which they must be wasted, is the right method of handling the problem and should be the goal to be aimed at ; but until that goal is attained, the unwanted forces are better run off through the natural channels, safeguarding the woman from undue child-bearing by the use of harmless methods of contraception. Of two evils choose the lesser : it is better to waste the life-force than have it turn to corruption.

Abortion is the murder of an unborn child, and is only justifiable in order to save the life of the mother. It must be remembered that life enters into the ovum at the moment of fertilisation, and it is none the less the vehicle of a living soul because it is microscopic. The incarnating ego is attached by subtle ties to the ovum over whose fertilisation it has presided, and is affected by any injury to its physical vehicle, however immature that vehicle may be ; though, of course, the injury is more serious after quickening takes place, at which time the ego enters its vehicle instead of overshadowing it as heretofore, an exoteric fact recognised by our common law.

An ego that has begun to incarnate and is violently turned back undergoes a severe shock and consequent suffering, to say nothing of the waste of time so caused, for birth is not nearly so simple a matter as death. When two people engage in the procreative act, they have set their hands to a bargain which includes right of entry for an ego should one desire to incarnate through them ; should an ego avail itself of this opportunity, they commit a serious offence against that soul if they destroy its vehicle, or should they, by the unjustifiable use of contraceptives deny entrance to egos, then they fail to discharge their obligations towards the Lord and Giver of Life.

CHAPTER XXIII

PROMISCUOUS INTERCOURSE AND UNNATURAL USE
OF THE SEX-FUNCTIONS

PROMISCUOUS sex-relations are not regarded lightly
by the occultist, because he well knows their consequences upon the inner planes and the causes they
set going in the unseen world.

The true value can only be obtained from the sex-
relationship by bringing all the seven bodies of
man into union, and this is a task, not merely for
a lifetime, but for an evolution. The tender affections, intellectual sympathies, and spiritual ideals
must all be mated, and this consummation cannot
be achieved save by long years of intimate companionship. The fleeting union can engage no more
than the senses, and effectually prevents a deeper
union being formed, because in each new relationship we have to begin all over again. We never
touch the higher planes save by fidelity.

Whenever we touch a soul as intimately as we do
in sexual intercourse, a karmic tie is made and a
rapport exists for a considerable time thereafter.
Therefore it is well to ask ourselves with what conditions we are establishing a rapport when entering

into such a union. Will the psychic forces that find entrance into racial consciousness through the channel opened up by a brothel prove beneficial to a soul when admitted to its innermost recesses ? Perhaps such considerations, were they more widely known, would serve to check the actions of those who are uninfluenced by the fact that their sensuality forces upon society a pariah caste which is denied all that makes life of any worth.

Concerning the unnatural forms of sexuality it is not customary to write save in books intended for the medical profession, but it is necessary to refer to them here, because they form, together with a knowledge of the power of certain drugs to affect consciousness, part of the stock-in-trade of black occultism. To be drawn by mystical cunning into a web of vile debauchery can scarcely be the object of a student of occultism, and he who seeks initiation into an occult fraternity had better be shrewdly observant, for not all fraternities serve the higher interests of humanity.

The Way of Initiation is not a scientific pursuit but a religion, and only the pure in heart can know God. Any tampering with morality is a danger-signal, and the neophyte should avoid any occultist whose life is not above reproach. The Kingdom of Heaven is not to be obtained at the price of a man's or woman's self-respect, nor can we hope to obtain any initiation that is of value by condoning evil. Unless a lodge is imbued by sufficiently high ideals to make it expel the unclean, keep out of it.

An occultist may deliberately devote himself to evil, or, through ignorance of the forces he is handling, he may get into the hands of evil, and in either case he is a danger to a neophyte. There are not many men in the Western esoteric tradition at the present time who are deliberately evil, not in the English lodges at any rate; but there are a very great many who are appallingly and disgracefully ignorant of that which they claim to teach, and they are just as dangerous, in fact more so, for a wicked man can be bought off or frightened off, but there is no means of appeal to a fool who is out of his depth.

Wherever drugs or sex are played with there is danger; the true occultist advances to a knowledge of the hidden side of things by spiritual intuition which is obtained by study, discipline, and purity of life.

Sexual perversion, so far as it concerns practical occultism, may be divided into two types—solitary stimulation of the generative organs and mutual stimulation by two people of the same sex.

In the first case, injury is inflicted upon the nervous system because there is an output of energy without any corresponding return through the medium of the etheric double, as described in the previous chapter. In addition to this, the energy thus put forth escapes into space, and is not returned

to the Divine, as it should be ; and if, as is almost
always the case, the act is accompanied by phantasy,
thought-forms are built upon the lower planes of
the unseen worlds, and these thought-forms are
liable to be ensouled by evil forces, and to become
active upon their own account, hanging about in the
neighbourhood of the place where they were
generated and influencing its atmosphere and all
persons who come into it, prompting them to
sensuality. These thought-forms are the incubi
and succubi of mediæval legend.

With regard to sexual stimulation between people
of the same sex, this is a well-known way, in conjunction with ritual, of producing occult development. It has been practised in the mysteries of
all races and ages in the periods of their decay, as
the records of ethnologists and historians show.
Two streams of force of the same type are called
forth, and naturally find no channels of return, as
the vehicles are both of the same polarity. These
forces are therefore available for magical purposes ;
hence the extensive use of what are commonly called
obscene practices as one of the easiest ways of
obtaining power. Something of the same lack of
scruple is shown when drugs are used to develop
clairvoyance. These things can be done, but there
is a price to pay, the price being that the person
so experimenting shall give himself over unre-
servedly to evil. If he attempt a divided allegiance,
he will develop what psychologists term conflict,
and mental breakdown will follow. It is more than

tragic that young boys should be foully made use of in black occultism. The public do not realise the significance of certain scandals that keep on cropping up, and therefore they do not take them sufficiently seriously.

CHAPTER XXIV

ABSTINENCE AND ASCETICISM

PEOPLE abstain from sexual intercourse for three reasons : firstly, because they are not in a position to meet the obligations so incurred; secondly, because sex inspires them with disgust; and thirdly, because they believe that asceticism is the path to spirituality.

With regard to the first reason, each man's conscience must be the arbiter, and a long step is taken upon the path when we sacrifice ourselves rather than injure another, even if we are impelled so to do by an error of judgment. With regard to the second, it is a case for a doctor, no healthy human being is so constituted; such repulsion is not a symptom of spirituality but of morbidity. A healthy mind is the only sound basis for spiritual development; it is morbid minds, when spiritual ambitions are grafted upon them, that give us Holy Inquisitions and Abodes of Love.

With regard to the third reason it is necessary to speak more fully, for physical austerity has ever been regarded by theologians as a *sine qua non* of spiritual advancement. It is a strange thought

that we can flatter God by condemning His handi-
work, for if he abhors sex, why did he create it ?
The Early Fathers reacted to the grossness of a
degenerate paganism with which they were sur-
rounded, and opposed extremes with extremes.
Frightened by licence they fled to aceticism. Few
men are great enough to transcend the civilisation
into which they are born, and many doctrines are
based upon the customs of a time rather than upon
universal principles, and so pass away with the
men for whose needs they were framed. The
relations between the sexes to-day, even at their
most earthly, are very different from those which
prevailed during the centuries in which the Church
was building up her traditions. The humanised
love of man and woman, of which physical passion
is but a part, was not the aspect of sex which
earned the condemnation of the Fathers, but the
cultivation of the animal till it outweighed the
human.

The occultist finds in the doctrine of the seven
planes the solution of the problem. For him each
plane has its place and its function, the second no
less than the seventh. Without the due development of each aspect of his sevenfold nature a man
cannot be made perfect ; it is to disproportion and
displacement that evil is due. There must be no
gap in the line of spiritual development ; a healthy
physical body and a healthy desire-body must be
the basis of a healthy mind, otherwise there can be
no clarity of spiritual vision. Initiation opens the

levels, plane by plane, and ignores none of them, and unless a man has developed within him the faculties which function upon each plane, he will miss its significance and fail to strike the full chord.

The esotericist disagrees with the theologian in that he says there should be full development of every aspect of man's nature, and that he should have full capacity for all human functions ; but he agrees with the theologian in saying that in certain aspects of the higher life there will be no sexual functioning. He refrains, however, from the exercise of such functions, not because he considers them evil, but because he requires the energy they would expend for other purposes.

The keynote of esoteric asceticism is the concentration of energy, not the avoidance of evil ; for the esotericist holds nothing evil which God has made, but right in its own time and place, and right for him too, however lofty his aspirations, at a certain phase of his development. He believes that a man must be fully and nobly human before he can hope to be superhuman. His asceticism is practised by directing the life-forces to those planes whereon he requires them, and inhibiting them from those on which he does not require them at the moment, not because such use would be evil, but because it would be wasteful. For his purpose he needs the most perfect self-control, a control so complete that he does not have to repress his desires, but feels no desire. Until he has gained

9

this mastery he cannot control the forces of the inner planes, which, if they were prematurely placed in his hands, would turn and rend him. Hence the secrecy which guards these forces, for on the plane of mind a thought is a thing and a mood is a place.

CHAPTER XXV

CONCLUSION

To the esotericist, sex in its sevenfold scope is of far greater significance than to the generality of mankind, to whom it is a temptation rather than a source of energy. He sees the life-force functioning in polarity upon every plane of existence, and no less sacred upon the lower than the higher. He approaches it with a fearlessness and even a familiarity that is seldom seen among his fellows, but he controls it with a strictness that is even more rare.

In these pages it has been my aim to show the reader that the higher aspects of the sex-nature are essential to the development of the perfect man, and to warn him of the dangers with which the ignorant handling of unseen forces may be attended.

A widespread interest in occult science has followed upon the great cataclysm through which we have recently passed. Many may pursue these studies for the sake of a new sensation, but more are in search of spiritual orientation; they desire to find a rock among the restless waters of appearance and opinion; their higher nature needs food which it cannot find in the world of men and things ; they seek, but know not what they seek for.

To these it may be said : Through all ages men have sought, and some have found ; there is a door through which we can pass out on to the higher planes, but that door is within the soul, it is an enlargement of consciousness whereby we perceive these things to which we have hitherto been blind, and from such perception comes the sense of reality which is lacking while we perceive nothing but appearances.   Whoso has this wider vision is freed from the limitations of the five physical senses ; his memory extends back beyond birth, and his hopes go forward beyond death ; he can perceive causes, and therefore has the gift of prophecy, and perceiving, he can often control.   Having all aspects of his own nature harmoniously developed, he is at one with all aspects of the universe, nothing is alien to him, and no form of existence is hostile. The path of life is open before him and he treads it with joy.   I who write have known these things.

END.

CPSIA information can be obtained
at www.ICGtesting.com
Printed in the USA
BVHW071121250520
580257BV00002B/287